German Literature

C. P. MAGILL

German Literature

OXFORD UNIVERSITY PRESS
London   Oxford   New York
1974

Oxford University Press, Ely House, London W. 1

GLASGOW NEW YORK TORONTO MELBOURNE WELLINGTON
CAPE TOWN IBADAN NAIROBI DAR ES SALAAM LUSAKA ADDIS ABABA
DELHI BOMBAY CALCUTTA MADRAS KARACHI LAHORE DACCA
KUALA LUMPUR SINGAPORE HONG KONG TOKYO

PAPERBACK ISBN 0 19 888063 4
CASEBOUND ISBN 0 19 885063 8

PRINTED IN GREAT BRITAIN
BY RICHARD CLAY (THE CHAUCER PRESS) LTD
BUNGAY, SUFFOLK

TO KATHLEEN

Preface

THIS book replaces and continues J. G. Robertson's *The Literature of Germany*, which appeared in the Home University Library in 1913. It is intended as a guide to some of the best works written in the German language from the Middle Ages to the present day and is in the nature of an anthology: the treatment of German literature has perforce been selective, the contents reflect the writer's taste and the limitations of his knowledge. I wish to acknowledge my debt, too heavy to be itemized, to all those critics and historians of German literature whose ideas I have appropriated and whose judgement has guided me. I also wish to thank those who have given me practical help in the preparation of the book.

It seemed pointless to try to say differently, and worse, what I have already said elsewhere as best I could, and so I have plagiarized myself here and there.

For the benefit of readers whose knowledge of the German language is slight. I have translated at the end of the book passages of German quoted in the text.

Aberystwyth, 1973   C. P. M.

Contents

1
The Middle Ages

GERMAN literature is troublesome material for those who like to make trim patterns out of untidy realities. Because of its richness and diversity, it fits awkwardly into a scheme of periods and movements. The disparate nature, the unstable history of the German-speaking peoples, now distributed over West and East Germany, Austria, and Switzerland, retarded the development of a standard language and gave their literature an erratic course; its history has been marked by spasmodic progression rather than measured evolution. Writers in the German language have rarely been supported, or constrained, by well-established native traditions and have veered, since they lacked this stabilizing influence, from one extreme to another; they have either set the pace or followed in the wake of literary fashion, striving to overhaul their contemporaries elsewhere in Europe. There have been notable phases of bold innovation, extreme individualism, challenging thought, and defiance of formal conventions, but it would be misleading to present these qualities as characteristic of German literature. Some of the greatest works in the German language were composed during a period in European literature, the Middle Ages, when conformity was a virtue, when authenticity was more prized than originality, and when the use of Romance models was respectable literary practice in Germany.

The best of medieval German literature was produced within the space of a few decades at the turn of the twelfth and thirteenth

centuries, towards the end, that is to say, of one of the great ages in
European civilization—the twelfth-century renascence. In what
followed and what came before there is no lack of linguistic,
historical, or antiquarian interest; what is missing is the broad
vision and the mastery of language which enable a great work to
withstand the passage of time. The impression of discontinuity
given by German literature in the Middle Ages is exaggerated by
the haphazard way in which much of it has reached us. The fragmentary *Hildebrandslied* (*The Song of Hildebrand*), probably
written down at the beginning of the ninth century, is the only rem-
nant of alliterative heroic poetry in German; while the old Germanic
legends must somehow have been kept alive in the intervening
period, we do not meet them again until we reach the *Nibelungenlied* (*The Song of the Nibelungs*), an epic written four hundred
years later. As for lyrical poetry, in which German literature is
especially rich, it gives the impression of emerging, Minerva-like,
fully mature in the twelfth century, although there is more evidence
here of a continuing native tradition.

The narrative poems and songs of medieval Germany—prose
literature was a much later development—were courtly in every
sense of the word. For the greater part they were composed by
knights from the lower ranks of the order of chivalry, for the entertainment of the Imperial and princely courts. They reflect the
chivalrous code of values, the ideals and fantasies of the international
military aristocracy which flourished during the period 1150–1250,
when the Holy Roman Empire, under the Hohenstaufen Emperors
Frederick I, Henry VI, and Frederick II, was at the summit of its
power. They were written in a courtly idiom, developed by the
poets of southern Germany and Austria in the eleventh century and
refined by their successors. It was a purely literary medium, short of
life and of limited currency, yet supple and vigorous. It gave the
poet a wealth of rhymes and rhythms, enabled him both to sustain a
long, eventful narrative or convey fine shades of feeling and thought,
accurately and tersely, in a love song. In the *Nibelungenlied*, in
Wolfram von Eschenbach's *Parzival* and Gottfried von Strassburg's
Tristan, in the verse of Walther von der Vogelweide—which serve
in this brief outline as a gateway to German literature—the poets

achieve, with the help of their supple medium, effects varying from the subtle to the stark and manoeuvre freely within the limits of courtly convention.

The *Nibelungenlied* was composed by an unknown Austrian poet at the turn of the twelfth and thirteenth centuries. Its traditional title, *The Song of the Nibelungs* and the more expressive alternative, *The Last Stand of the Nibelungs*, are both derived from the last lines of manuscripts of the poem. The poet has a good story to tell and tells it well, except for his cavalier treatment of details. His Nibelungs, when we first meet them, are a warrior race from a northern land but for reasons best known to himself he merges them towards the end of this story with the Rhineland Burgundians, whose downfall forms the climax of the poem. The *Nibelungenlied* is a blend of the genteel and the primitive, the grotesque and the terrible, of chivalrous ideals and barbaric deeds. It is as if an archaic statue had fallen into the hands of a renovator who smoothes out some of its crudities but is unwilling to soften its grim features. The author worked within a tradition of Germanic heroic poetry rooted in the fifth or sixth century; his raw material was an amalgam of historical legend and myth embedded in Norse and Germanic lays and his sources included a lost epic on the destruction of the Nibelungs, written in the mid-twelfth century. The disaster or, not to put too fine a point on it, the butchery with which the *Nibelungenlied* ends goes back to the massacre in the fifth century of the Burgundian King Gundaharius and his kinsmen by a Hunnish army, led, according to legend, by Attila. This event became entwined over the centuries with tales of murder and revenge, of a Nibelung treasure and of two superhuman figures, the Amazonian Queen Brunhild of Iceland and the Netherlandish hero Siegfried. Siegfried had the strength of Hercules and the near-invulnerability of Achilles. His murder is at the heart of the *Nibelungenlied* and two of his exploits have a bearing on its action: he killed two Nibelung princes, made himself master of their nebulous realm, and took their treasure of red gold; he killed the dragon Fafnir and, having bathed in its blood, got a hide of impenetrable horniness, except at one point on his back where a leaf fell during his gory baptism.

The *Nibelungenlied* was intended to be sung or chanted (the exact mode is uncertain) to a courtly audience and is written in four-line strophes, gnarled and inflexible but well suited to the story. It consists of thirty-nine episodes or 'âventiuren' and resembles in its structure a massive drama in two acts—the first ending in a treacherous murder, the second in the annihilation of two armies, the link between them the enduring hatred of a vengeful woman. The action spans nearly forty years and covers much ground. The first part takes us to Worms in the Rhineland, where the Burgundian King Gunther, his two brothers, and his sister Kriemhild hold court, to the court of King Sigmund and his son Siegfried in the Netherlands, to the court of Queen Brunhild at Isenstein, and to Nibelungenland, where Siegfried claims his treasure and raises an army of a thousand vassals. The roots of the final disaster lie in a double marriage—between Siegfried and Kriemhild, Gunther and Brunhild—and in the events which precede and accompany them. Siegfried not only wins Brunhild for Gunther, whose prowess is less than heroic, but stands in for him as husband after his humiliating wedding night. Siegfried contents himself in this version of the tale with filching Brunhild's ring and girdle, but for all the good this restraint does him he might as well have consummated the marriage for Gunther. Ten years later, Brunhild, with Gunther's connivance, instigates the murder of Siegfried by Hagen, the strong man of the Burgundian court. In the second part, the scene shifts from the Rhine to the Danube and the land of the Huns. After thirteen years of widowhood and a token reconciliation with her brother Gunther, Kriemhild marries King Etzel (Attila) and lives with him for a further thirteen years in Hungary, still nursing her hatred for Gunther and Hagen. Her revenge, when she finally takes it, is terrible. Invited to a feast at Etzel's court, the Burgundians are penned up in his great hall, which Kriemhild orders to be set on fire, and are put to the sword. At the end, only Gunther and Hagen are left standing. When they are overcome by Etzel's guest, Dietrich of Verona, Kriemhild has Gunther executed, while she herself beheads Hagen with Siegfried's sword, only to be cut in pieces by Dietrich's outraged vassal Hildebrand.

There is no mystery about *what* is done in the *Nibelungenlied*; *why* it is done is another matter. Like all epics of the period, the

Nibelungenlied is full of pitfalls—particularly where motive is concerned—for those who, unversed in medieval lore, perforce bring to it no more than their own twentieth-century outlook, taste, and sensibility. While our medieval forbears were not creatures from another planet, they were not facsimiles of ourselves and when we read their poetry we are liable to miss or misconstrue vital nuances of thought and feeling. Moreover, the conventions followed by the medieval story-teller differed radically from those of the modern novelist or script-writer and are the cause of many a real or apparent obscurity or inconsistency. If we find much that is puzzling in the *Nibelungenlied*, we can take comfort from the knowledge that it has perplexed generations of scholars and that its implications are still being debated.

The poet is of little help to us. Although he can be garrulous when he chooses, he is tight-lipped about what we would consider essentials. He ends with a colourless tag about the impermanence of joy, which must ever turn to sorrow at the finish, and leaves us to make what we will of his story. Unlike Richard Wagner, who entangled the destinies of gods and men in his cycle of heroic operas, *Der Ring des Nibelungen*, the poet of the *Nibelungenlied* operates in a religious vacuum. Christian Providence plays no part in the proceedings and there is no more than a hint of a malign Fate at work. The German poet Klabund read his own situation into the epic when he wrote, shortly after the end of the Great War: 'Have we not all experienced the *Nibelungenlied* in our own bodies and souls? An inescapable fate has involved us, guilty and innocent alike, in a common disaster, and a world has fallen in ruins.' The impression we get nowadays of the *Nibelungenlied* depends on where we focus our eyes—on one or other of the outstanding characters perhaps, on Kriemhild, turned monster out of intemperate love, or on Hagen, that ruthless, sagacious, but ultimately calamitous soldier-politician, or on the struggle for power between them. Wherever we look, we are left with a sense of the flimsiness of civilized life. As the story moves to its climax, the courtly festivities, ceremonies, and tourneys are lost to view, the fine clothing and the knightly accoutrements fall away and we are left with a sight of man as the most ferocious of all animals.

(2)

Wolfram von Eschenbach's *Parzival* (*c.* 1210) takes us into an altogether different world—the world of Arthurian legend, originally created by the Celtic imagination but here seen through a characteristically German pair of eyes. Up to the middle of the twelfth century, the fabulous tales centred on Arthur and his court were the preserve of the Celtic fringe, ignored or despised by the historians and writers of the European heartland; they entered the mainstream of European literature thanks to the success of Geoffrey of Monmouth's Latin *History of the Kings of Britain*, that 'shameless and audacious work of fiction', as it has been aptly called. Geoffrey's crude but colourful account of his hero Arthur and his valiant warriors proved a rich mine for the poets and prose writers of the later twelfth and early thirteenth centuries. Had Geoffrey not given them Arthur, they would doubtless have found some other hero— possibly Charlemagne—who could be used to give coherence and ethical substance to their tales of knight-errantry and romantic love. As it was, the Arthurian legend gave them precisely what they wanted—a nucleus of material which could be moulded to suit the conventions of the age of chivalry and which was, moreover, readily expandable. As far as *Parzival* is concerned, the most significant addition to the legend was the motif of the Holy Grail—either the dish used by Christ and the Apostles at the Last Supper or the cup in which his blood was caught when the Roman lance pierced his side or, according to Wolfram's eccentric view of it, a stone with miraculous properties brought down to earth by the angels who remained neutral in the heavenly war between God and Lucifer. The Grail served a double purpose in Arthurian romance; it supplied a meaningful goal for the quests undertaken by the knights of the Round Table and it enabled the story-teller to accommodate the code of the military aristocracy to the Christian ethos of medieval society. (In *Parzival*, the hero has a footing both in the Arthurian Order of chivalry and in the related, but more exalted Order of the Grail.)

It was by way of France that the Arthurian legend, stripped of its Celtic character, passed into Germany. The chief agent in the development of the cycle of Arthurian stories was Chrétien de

Troyes, the source used by Wolfram's contemporary Hartmann von Aue for his two Arthurian epics *Erec* and *Iwein*. Chrétien's writings included a *Perceval* or *Conte del Graal*, but what this mundane and unmystical poet would ultimately have made of Sir Percival and the Grail we cannot tell, for he left his epic unfinished. Wolfram not only finished it for him, but so tranformed and spiritualized it that he felt obliged to cite, or invent, a second source, the unidentifiable Provençal poet Kyot, to justify his innovations. Unconventional enough in other ways, he shared it seems, the scruples about authenticity and the unease about originality peculiar to the poets of his time.

Parzival is a lengthy and elaborate allegory of spiritual conflict, a medieval *Pilgrim's Progress*—for it tallies with the description of his purpose which Bunyan gave in his apology to the reader:

> This book, it chalketh out before thine eyes
> The man that seeks the everlasting prize:
> It shews you whence he comes, whither he goes,
> What he leaves undone, also what he does;
> It shews you how he runs, and runs,
> 'Till he unto the Gate of Glory comes.

Parzival is, of course, a more specialized kind of pilgrim than Bunyan's Christian. He comes of a race of knights and moves in a knightly society; his progress is towards a synthesis of knightly virtue and service to God. A man, Wolfram tells us in his epilogue, who can keep his soul intact and at the same time win renown, who can please both God and the World, has not lived his life in vain. Nevertheless, Parzival is not a totally exceptional being, remote from the generality of mankind. This seems to be the implication of Wolfram's admittedly ambiguous prologue, with its references to the sin of 'zwível' (despair and inconstancy) and the virtue of 'unverzaget mannes muot' (steadfastness). Although Parzival may not be Everyman, he has at his best a family resemblance to Bunyan's Mr. Great-Heart, the slayer of Giant Despair and the demolisher of Doubting-Castle.

Wolfram describes Parzival summarily as 'bold of heart but slow to wisdom'. We first meet him as a guileless innocent, brought up in sylvan solitude by his mother, Herzeloyde, so that he may escape the fate of his adventurous and feckless father, Gahmuret of Anjou, who came to an untimely end in the service of the Caliph of Baghdad, leaving a pair of widows, the one Moorish, the other—Parzival's mother—Welsh. Despite her precautions, Parzival is drawn, by Providence masquerading as chance, to Arthur's court and takes up the chivalrous life, unaware that he is the rightful heir to the Kingdom of the Grail. He comes into his Kingdom by a devious route, by way of uncouth blunders, unpremeditated sins, and a period in the spiritual wilderness, consumed by hatred of God. Whether his salvation is due to divine grace, predestination, or a conscious effort of will, to good luck or good judgement or a combination of the two, is left unclear, together with much else in the epic.

So scanty is our knowledge of Wolfram that we have to take the risk of deducing his personality from his writings. As the narrator of *Parzival* he assumes a stance of rugged individualism, claims that he is illiterate, and professes contempt, as befits an 'upstanding man', for the bookish and sedentary trade of poet. He uses the normal medium of the medieval German epic, the short rhyming couplet, but his way of manipulating it puts him in a class of his own. The structure of *Parzival* is complex—the hero's friend and, possibly, *alter ego* Gawan plays a major part in it. The grave subject is set off by touches of irreverent humour, the symbolism by vivid word-pictures; the thought is capricious, the language condensed and involved. Wolfram is not the easiest of poets; even his contemporary Gottfried von Strassburg, better placed than ourselves to get his drift, found him obscure. The spiritual counsel and explanation of the Grail given to Parzival by his uncle, the hermit Trevrizent, bring to mind those 'sermons by mystical Germans who preach from ten to four' recommended by the Mikado as a punishment for habitual bores. The reality of Wolfram's Christian faith is unquestionable. If his epic has a weakness, it is that like other religious allegories it invites unflattering comparisons with the great originals on which his faith is based. *Parzival*, it has been said, depicts the struggle of Man with God. If this be so, and if we are not to find it merely fanciful, we have to shut out of our minds all memories of the splendour and profundity of the Book of Job.

(3)

Wear me as a seal upon your heart,
   as a seal upon your arm,
for love is strong as death,
passion cruel as the grave;
   it blazes up like blazing fire,
   fiercer than any flame.
Many waters cannot quench love,
   no flood can sweep it away;
if a man were to offer for love
   the whole wealth of his house,
   it would be utterly scorned

—the Bridegroom's acknowledgement, in *The Song of Songs*, of the power of love could serve as a motto for Gottfried von Strassburg's *Tristan*. Stripped of its embellishments, it is a tale of passionate and irresistible love, heedless of moral scruples, legal obligations, and personal loyalties, ending in disaster. Engrossing in its own right, the work of a well-stocked and lucid mind, it takes on a deeper shade of interest if we see it in the setting of its time. In modern literature, no holds are barred in the handling of love and forbidden love has lost its potency as a subject, but when Gottfried wrote his anatomy of adultery the Church was at the height of its influence and sexual behaviour was regulated by powerful sanctions, ecclesiastical and social. To read *Tristan* today is to marvel at the ingenuity with which Gottfried avoids the moral quicksands in his path.

The story of Tristan and Isolde, or Tristram and Yseult as we know them in English, was of Celtic origin and had suffered various sea-changes by the time it reached Gottfried. His source was the French *Tristan*, written in the mid-twelfth century by the poet he calls Thomas of Britain, who gave a courtly gloss to early versions of the tale. Gottfried never completed his epic and the finale has to be supplied from Thomas's version (of which, by a happy accident, the last part has survived) or from the German poets who continued the story in the thirteenth and fourteenth centuries.

Gottfried begins with an account of Tristan's parentage in which there already were ominous signs of the devastating force of love. He is the son, conceived out of wedlock, of Rivalin of Parmenie, who elopes with Blancheflor, the sister of King Mark of Cornwall. Shortly after their marriage, Rivalin is killed in battle and Blancheflor dies in childbirth. The orphan Tristan is brought up by Rivalin's marshal Rual and comes to the court of his uncle, King Mark, by an odd set of circumstances. Kidnapped by Norse pirates, he is landed on the Cornish coast after a violent storm—which Gottfried implausibly, in view of its dire consequences, passes off as an act of God. Tristan's identity is established, Mark makes him his heir and he is created a knight. He has all the necessary qualifications: even in boyhood, his accomplishments were prodigious; hunting, fencing, languages, chess, and music—he is master of them all; he is, moreover, valorous in combat, exquisite in manner, and comely of figure. He would be dull literary stuff were he not also a fluent liar and a master of disguise, with a natural talent for dissimulation and a singular lack of conscience, at least after love has him in its grip. He encounters Princess Isolde (Isolde the Fair) half-way through the epic. He acts as a marriage broker on the second of two expeditions to Ireland and arranges a *mariage de convenance* between Isolde and King Mark. It is on the journey back to Cornwall with Isolde that the accident happens which alters the course of their lives. They drink in error the potion intended by the Queen of Ireland as a guarantee of her daughter's successful marriage, and by the end of the voyage are irredeemably in love. Gottfried is at his best in his account of their subsequent life at court—their cunning deceptions and amorous intrigues, their banishment, forgiveness, and return, the efforts of Mark to preserve some shred of dignity in his impossible situation. His narrative breaks off with Tristan, who has taken flight and entered the service of the Duke of Arundel, on the point of marriage with the Duke's daughter, a second and second-best Isolde, Isolde of the White Hands.

In the finale of Thomas of Britain's poem, Tristan, in the course of a chivalrous adventure, is wounded in the loins by a poisoned lance and sends across the sea for Isolde the Fair, who alone can heal him. Contrary winds delay her and Tristan, tricked by his jealous wife into believing that she is not on the returning ship, dies before she can reach him. She takes her lover in her arms and dies at his side.

Such is the bare outline of a story clothed by Gottfried in a finely worked fabric of poetry. He is much more 'literary' than the other epic poets of the time; alone among them, he seems to love words and ideas for their own sake; he plays with them, decks them out with the considerable range of rhetorical devices at his finger-tips. He has a distinctive style; his verse is fluent, his transitions neat, the pace of his narrative artfully varied. He is concerned to express himself as elegantly as possible and only rarely does he labour a point. Although he is clear in details, in larger matters he is an elusive writer with a marked vein of irony in his disposition. He is thus open to all manner of interpretations. If we are to take at their face value his prologue and the disquisitions on love which pepper his narrative, we are invited to regard Tristan and Isolde as an exemplary pair and the story as a celebration of perfect, absolute, or total love. He addresses himself to an all too scanty band of 'noble hearts', prepared to accept love in its fullness, its pain as well as its bliss, and count not only the world but heaven too well lost for it. Love is its own world: 'Let me be part of it,' says Gottfried, 'and let me be damned or saved with it.' It has been wisely observed that he behaves towards his lovers like an advocate towards his clients; he presents them in the best possible light and leaves the question of guilt or innocence to the jury. He is, of course, a guileful advocate, and pleads diminished responsibility. He puts the onus of blame upon the fateful love-potion and to a lesser extent on the obtuse Mark and has selected a packed jury of 'noble hearts'. His eloquence is coloured by a vague and disarming religiosity. Lest the 'Minnegrotte', the lovers' cave in which Tristan and Isolde live during their banishment in blissful solitude, should too closely resemble a pagan temple—the bed is dedicated to the Goddess of Love—its structure is described in allegorical terms appropriate to a Christian church. He turns the tables on those twelfth-century mystics who used sexual imagery to denote the union of the soul with God and he uses their language to denote his own kind of ideal love. It transcends the unheroic and debased sexual ethics of his day, which he denounces, but it is neither exclusively nor mainly spiritual. If his

account of the tender relations between Tristan and Isolde is re-
strained by our standards, it is far from mealy-mouthed. Their love
is as much a union of kindred bodies as a marriage of true minds.

Faint and distorted echoes of the *Nibelungenlied*, *Parzival*, and
Tristan can still be heard in the music-dramas of Richard Wagner.
Wagner, who wrote his own libretti, used chiefly Icelandic and
Norwegian sources for *The Ring*; when composing his *Parsifal* he
found Wolfram's version useless for his purpose and transformed
the story to suit his needs; his *Tristan and Isolde* bears some relation to Gottfried's *Tristan* but, like *Parsifal*, it is coloured by his
personal experience and by his quasi-religious doctrine (influenced
by the pessimism of Schopenhauer) of suffering, renunciation, and
redemption.

(4)

The lyrical poet and the song-writer would be lost without love;
fulfilled, or more commonly unrequited, it is the staple of their
craft. It was the dominant theme of the medieval German lyric and
the sole theme, endlessly varied, of 'Minnesang'. 'Minnesang', the
German form of the love poetry developed by the troubadours of
Provence and the trouvères of northern France, was an inbred art,
practised in its heyday by courtiers for the entertainment of courtiers,
an accomplishment demanding both musical and literary skill. The
Minnesinger composed both the text and the melody of his songs
and although most of the melodies have been lost, enough have
survived to make clear the intricacy of the complete 'Minnelied'.
Metrical structure and melody were combined in patterns which
were the poet-composer's chief means of displaying his inventiveness; his text gave him limited scope for originality because of the
conventions which controlled it. 'Minnesang' was grounded on that
notion of courtly love which was one of the oddest products of the
medieval imagination. Its origins are obscure and a variety of
explanations—among them the influence of Arabic love-poetry of
the tenth and eleventh centuries and the cult of the Virgin Mary
—have been suggested for the idealized view of womanhood which
colours it. The relation of suitor to mistress in the 'Minnelied'
undoubtedly reflects the fealty owed by a vassal to his lord in the

feudal system. The suitor's love, in courtly song of the more austere kind, takes the form of devoted service, without hope of return or fear of calumny, to an obdurate lady, inaccessible because she is married or socially superior, or both. A more rewarding, but precarious kind of love is celebrated in the 'Tagelied' or dawn-song, a variant of 'Minnesang' found in many literatures; after a night together, the lovers awaken to harsh reality and part at daybreak. The best of the Minnesingers, among them Reinmar von Hagenau, the leading poet at the Viennese court towards the end of the twelfth century and the Thuringian poet Heinrich von Morungen, operate adroitly within their field of convention. Reinmar was the classic exponent of 'Minnesang'; praise of women, the dilemma of the lover, desiring both to maintain his lady on her pedestal and bring her down to earth—these are his constant themes. His songs are an intellectual exploration of love but like a good politician he creates an illusion of simplicity and spontaneity. Heinrich von Morungen is a more vigorous and less plaintive suitor; his imagery is bolder, his feeling more directly expressed, his love more of an elemental force; a substantial personality rather than a disembodied talent can be sensed at work in his songs.

'Minnesang' was a literary fashion with a comparatively short life; nevertheless, in the centuries to come German poets were well served by the idiom devised for the handling of love by song-writers like Reinmar, Heinrich von Morungen, and the ablest of them all, Walther von der Vogelweide.

'For forty years or more I sang of love'—so Walther von der Vogelweide tells us in a late poem. In fact, Walther sang of much more than love; he wrote in addition to his 'Minnelieder' religious and political songs and a substantial amount of verse which can broadly be described as sententious. None of his contemporaries can match his amplitude and variety; he writes with an ease and assurance which we do not encounter again in German poetry until we reach Goethe in the eighteenth century. Only six complete specimens of his melodies have survived, but his songs do not need the support of music; the best of them are so humane in content and clear in structure that no more than a linguistic barrier stands between them and the modern reader.

Walther lived by his wits and his talent; born into the knightly class and a cut above a minstrel, he was dependent on the bounty of lay and ecclesiastical patrons. He learnt his art in Vienna, led a wandering existence in his middle years, and was rewarded late in life with the grant of a fief by the Emperor Friedrich II. As a propagandist of pliant loyalty but consistent principles of the patriotic sort he was involved in the struggle between Empire and Papacy which bedevilled German history in the Middle Ages and in the contention between the houses of Welf and Hohenstaufen for the Imperial throne. On the evidence of his poetry, he was an awkward but loyal member of the German courtly establishment; he was sensitive to the charge of boorishness levelled against it and posed as the champion of German manners and German womanhood; in religion he was orthodox and in matters of taste he took the part of decorum. His poetry, however, is far from conservative. In his most memorable group of love-songs he broke away from the basic convention of 'Minnesang' and substituted for the inaccessible lady of high degree a lowlier, more compliant, and full-blooded kind of mistress. Submissive yearning and high-minded resistance make way for a love given and taken on equal terms. The feelings voiced by the girl in the pastourelle beginning

> Under der linden
> an der heide
> dâ unser zweier bette was

are as fresh and natural as the setting in which she encounters her lover.

In poems like 'Under der linden' Walther reverted to an earlier tradition of German love-song. In his sententious and political verse he developed another well-established type of poetry—the 'Spruch', a pithy didactic song embodying a piece of homespun wisdom or a religious truth. Nowadays we can take a disinterested pleasure in his political songs, in his caustic treatment of Pope Innocent III, his way of intertwining his private concerns and public issues, of wrapping up his partisan views in lofty, inoffensive platitudes. In his 'Reichston', a song written in support of Philip of Swabia, he arouses expectations of profundity by depicting himself in an attitude like that of Rodin's 'Penseur':

> Ich saz ûf eime steine
> und dahte bein mit beine;
> dar ûf satzte ich den ellenbogen,
> ich hete in mîne hand gesmogen
> daz kinne und ein mîn wange.

He laments the disorderly state of the realm which makes it hard to achieve honour and wealth without forfeiting divine grace; back the right candidate for the throne, he implies, and God and Mammon will be simultaneously served. In the poem, possibly his swan-song, beginning

> Owê war sint verswunden alliu mîniu jâr!
> ist mir mîn leben getroumet, oder ist ez wâr?

he shows himself a master of the art of modulation. He starts off on an elegiac note; rueful reflections on his past life, those vanished years which now seem no more than a dream, lead into a doleful commentary upon the joyless and decadent age and the short-comings of the younger generation, anxiety-ridden, uncouth in behaviour, slovenly in dress. In the last strophe there is a neat change of key and a switch to the theme on which Walther was no doubt commissioned to write his song—the unhallowed but successful Crusade undertaken by Friedrich II in 1227. He calls the German knights to arms, touches on the vanity of earthly joy, reminds them that the world, many-coloured on the surface, is black as death with-in, and assures them that a crown of eternal bliss awaits them if they take part in the Crusade. If only I could accompany you overseas, he concludes, a shade implausibly, the burden of my song would not be 'Woe is me!'

(5)

In the dissonant and satirical dance-songs of Neidhart von Reuen-thal, which outraged Walther's sense of good form, there are clear signs that the courtly convention was breaking down. Neidhart, who is accounted the last of the great medieval German poets, cannot on the available evidence have outlived the middle of the thirteenth century. His successors were content to re-work old forms or themes and were it not for the folk-songs of anonymous composers the fourteenth and fifteenth centuries would be thinly represented in anthologies of German verse. The later Middle Ages were a barren period in European literature—in France and in England (except for the age of Chaucer) no less than in Germany. Whatever the reasons—the shift of cultural activity from the courts to the towns and Imperial cities and linguistic fragmentation were among them—German literature during this period, and far beyond it, lagged behind the arts of sculpture, painting, music, and architecture. The chief impediment to the growth of prose writing in the vernacular was the dominance of Latin as the language of Church, State, and learning. The best known of all medieval German works, *The Imitation of Christ*, a book more widely translated than any other save the Bible, was written in Latin early in the fifteenth century and is usually attributed to the Augustinian canon Thomas à Kempis, named after his birthplace, Kempen in the Lower Rhineland. His *Imitatio Christi* is an example of German 'Innerlichkeit' at its best, disciplined by the medium in which it is expressed and by the aims which it serves; the lucid and unadorned prose reflects the purity of mind and simplicity of purpose commended by Thomas in his 'Counsels of the Inner Life'. His predecessors, the Dominican mystics of the fourteenth century, were less notable for clarity than for their pursuit of a language to express the inexpressible. The greatest of them, Meister Eckhart, enriched the German vocabulary with abstract philosophical terms and created an idiom, often cloudy and ambiguous, for the communication of spiritual experience which had a lasting influence on German style. Medieval German prose was conditioned by the religious climate of the age; its most conspicuous landmark, *Der Ackermann*, commonly known as *Der Ackermann aus Böhmen* (*The Ploughman of Bohemia*), lies on the boundary between theology and imaginative literature.

Der Ackermann was written shortly after 1400, probably by Johann von Tepl, a Bohemian scholar and notary in whose lifetime Prague was the capital of the Empire and Bohemia the point of entry of Italian humanism into Imperial territory. It is a dialogue between a bereaved husband and Death, a disputation in which plaintiff and defendant argue their cause before God as the supreme arbiter. The emotional impulse behind it was the author's grief at the death of his first wife and in one sense it is a memorial to her; in a larger sense, it records a spiritual conflict, a struggle to reconcile the brute fact of death with belief in the goodness of God. It was also meant, improbable as it may seem, as a stylistic exercise, a cold-blooded attempt to reproduce the subtleties of Latin rhetoric in the German vernacular. It is studded with figures of speech and the title itself is a metaphor. 'I call myself a ploughman; my quill is my plough,' the author tells us, and sets off without further explanation to plough his crooked furrow. He begins with an outburst of grief, a denunciation of Death, but it is soon diverted into a battle of wits with his formidable opponent. He is up against a master of dialectic, unyielding, but compassionate, who justifies his place in the divine scheme of things with unassailable logic and scathing irony. In delivering judgement, God chides both parties for pitching their claims too high, but pronounces the battle well fought and not with-out sense; he gives the victory to Death and offers the Ploughman the consolation of honourable defeat. The epilogue, like the rest of *Der Ackermann*, is an odd blend of pedantry and passion. It begins with the Ploughman's prayer to God, a fulsome eulogy, stiff with conventional and far-fetched epithets; it ends with a brief and moving prayer for the soul of his dead wife. Nothing quite like *Der Ackermann* had been written before in German; Johann von Tepl exploits the resources of the language, controls the ebb and flow of the argument, and directs it towards its resolution with exceptional skill. Although the battle is won by Death; it is a close-run thing and the final impression made on us is far from sombre; the Ploughman counters Death's gloomy, life-denying doctrine with eloquent arguments touched by the spirit of humanism. Listening to the disputants, we seem to move back and forth in time, ending up in that twilit zone between the Middle Ages and the Renaissance.

2

The Sixteenth and Seventeenth Centuries

(1)

THE Renaissance is commonly considered a turning-point in European civilization: the rebirth of the ethos of classical antiquity, the rediscovery of the human personality, the release of imprisoned intellectual energies—these are among the associations, suggestive of unexampled spiritual buoyancy, which have collected around it. Whereas the Renaissance has a prominent place in Italian, French, and English literary history, its influence on Germany is much less conspicuous; it is clearer in the Latin writings of the humanists than in the vernacular literature which is our concern. Its impact on Germany was blunted by the Reformation, by the divisive wars and ideological ferment which accompanied it in the sixteenth century. Nothing written during this turbulent and complex age gives us as sharp an insight into its temper as the graphic art of Albrecht Dürer; the mood of Germany on the eve of the Reformation is made visible in his *Apocalypse* (the early series of woodcuts, full of portentous visions, illustrating the Revelation of St. John) and in the three 'master engravings' he made after his second visit to Italy—*The Knight, Death, and the Devil, St. Jerome in his Study*, and the enigmatic *Melancholia I*. In the last of these the figure of Melancholy, grave and inward-looking, is surrounded, not by the emblems of mortality or despondency one might expect but by symbols of human endeavour and the new learning; *Melancholia* bespeaks a deep spiritual unease, the more striking because it is expressed through harmonious classical form.

In the sixteenth century, many of the best minds in Germany operated on the fringe of literature. Their energies were channelled either into practical scholarship—the business of editing and translating and the study of Greek and Hebrew—or into religious controversy. In the wordy battles of the Reformation, satire was a favourite weapon of the disputants. It was more notable for its rancour than its wit and in point of crudity there is little to choose between the disputants. *Von dem großen Lutherischen Narren* (*The Great Lutheran Fool*), by the Franciscan monk Thomas Murner, is a singularly scurrilous lampoon, but then Luther himself was a master of inelegant invective. These uncharitable exchanges recall Samuel Butler's comment on the English sectarians of the seventeenth century:

> To fight for Truth is but the sole dominion
> Of every idiot's humour or opinion

and it is with relief that one turns back a little in time to the more urbane and entertaining satire of Sebastian Brant.

Brant's *Das Narrenschiff* (*The Ship of Fools*) was written in 1494, went through many editions in the sixteenth century, was translated into English and French and was the first vernacular work (it was in Alemannic) to become widely known outside German-speaking territory. The first edition was a handsome book, illustrated with woodcuts, published in Basel by one of the presses which sprang up in Switzerland and Germany after the invention, in the mid-fifteenth century, of printing by movable metal type. The author was a new species of literary animal; a townsman, university trained—he was for a time lecturer in jurisprudence in Basel and moved in humanistic circles—and a man of affairs; during the last twenty years of his life he was town clerk of Strassburg, his birthplace. His panorama of human folly has a traditional framework. The central idea of the book, the identification of sin and folly, is well rooted in medieval thought and the ship which houses his foolish company is based on the floats used in carnival processions. We never learn what happens to the ship, which presumably founders on its voyage to Narragonien, the Land of Fools, under the direction of its idiotic helmsman. What Brant gives us is an inconsequential catalogue, drawn up in rhyming couplets, of miscellaneous follies, some timeless, some contemporary, reflecting the social and moral changes afoot in his day. Mortal sins, venial vices, fashionable addictions like gambling and dancing follow each other in quick succession. Brant laments the decline of faith and the anarchy into which the Empire has sunk. He works his way through all the estates of the realm: self-seeking princes, slothful priests, unscrupulous merchants, usurers, price-manipulators and monopolists, ostentatious peasants and work-shy artisans, discontented with their station in life. He attacks trendy theologians, pretentious scholars, and the pursuit of superfluous knowledge; he gives pride of place in his ship to the 'Büchernarr', the Bookish Fool, who sits on the prow, like a travesty of Dürer's Melancholia, surrounded by his useless library. His humanism is no more than skin-deep and hardly goes beyond a parade of classical allusions. Brant may hold up Socrates as a model of sanity, but the Bible is for him the true fount of wisdom, a sufficient guide to right conduct in an unstable and perplexing world. His satire is neither malicious nor self-righteous; he signs himself disarmingly 'der Narr Sebastianus Brant' and speaks as a fool grown conscious of his folly, in the familiar tones of an old-fashioned conservative dismayed by the infirmity of the modern age.

Despite the troubled times, a popular literature of great diversity —and uneven quality—flourished in sixteenth-century Germany. If the best poetry of the period is to be found in ballads, folk-song, and Lutheran hymns, 'Meistergesang' undoubtedly provides the most tedious. The Mastersingers, most of them members of the craft guilds, applied manufacturing techniques to verse-making and achieved extraordinary levels of productivity. The best known of them, the Nürnberg master-shoemaker Hans Sachs, achieved an output of over 4,000 'Meisterlieder' and nearly 2,000 plays and dramatic anecdotes—precious material for the social historian but sadly deficient in memorable lines. Alongside undistinguished prose romances, many of them translated from the French, we find chapbooks like *Ein kurtzweilig lesen von Dyl Ulenspiegel* (*A Diverting*

Account of Till Eulenspiegel), (1515) and *Historia von D. Johann Fausten*, featuring characters who have passed into German literary mythology.

The author of the *History of Dr. Johann Faustus*, published in Frankfurt in 1587, concealed his identity but made his purpose explicit in his elaborate title-page. His account of the adventures and exploits of the notorious necromancer who sold himself to the Devil for a prescribed period of years—'bis er endlich seinen wol verdienten Lohn empfangen' (until he got what was coming to him)—was intended as an awful example and sincere warning to all arrogant and godless men. It was a true story, he assured his readers, put together from Faust's personal papers. His Faust is a clever man, Doctor of Theology of the University of Wittenberg, who degenerates into a quack doctor, astrologer, and practitioner of black magic. Thirsty for forbidden knowledge, full of high-flown, devilish thoughts, he makes a pact with Mephistopheles and for a term of twenty-four years performs magical feats, makes fantastic voyages, and enjoys boundless sensual pleasures, including a liaison with Helen of Troy. When the day of reckoning is near, Faust summons his students, makes a clean breast of his sins, and warns them of his impending death. Entering his room the next morning, they find the walls spattered with blood and brains, the only other vestiges of their professor being his eyes and some of his teeth, and after a prolonged search locate his mutilated corpse lying on a dunghill. After this horrific description of Faust's well-deserved end, the author exhorts the reader to renounce the Devil and all his works, and finishes with a quotation from Luther's version of the First Epistle of Peter: 'Be sober, be watchful; your adversary the devil, as a roaring lion, walketh about, seeking whom he may devour; whom withstand, steadfast in your faith.'

The History of Dr. Faustus has a strong Lutheran flavour and its author, of whom nothing is known, may well have been a Lutheran cleric. His original, in so far as he can be reconstructed from the legends which collected around him, was a disreputable charlatan and the Faustus of the chap-book is an unheroic figure. His stiff-necked pride of intellect, his revolt against divine authority gave him, however, a symbolic quality which was exploited first by

Christopher Marlowe in *The Tragical History of Dr. Faustus*, and subsequently by a long line, extending to our own day, of German writers. Marlowe based his play on the first English translation of the chap-book, the *History of the Damnable Life and Deserved Death of Dr. John Faustus*; while he was the first to raise Faust to tragic stature, he remains true, at least in his final chorus, to the spirit of the original story:

> Faustus is gone: regard his hellish fall,
> Whose fiendful fortune may exhort the wise,
> Only to ponder at unlawful things,
> Whose deepness doth entice such forward wits
> To practise more than heavenly power permits.

By the time the *History of Dr. Faustus* appeared, Martin Luther had been dead for forty years and the Reformation had run its course, with consequences of a gravity he cannot have foreseen. Luther is so big a figure that a thumb-nail sketch of him would be an absurdity and no more than a reference to his translation of the Bible, completed in 1534, is possible here. It was an extraordinary linguistic feat: Luther took as his guide the language spoken by 'the mother in the home, the children in the streets, and the ordinary man in the market-place' and turned the Bible into plain German, aiming above all at clarity and precision. His versions of books like Ecclesiastes or The Song of Songs, compared with those in the English Authorised Version of 1611 (the work of a team of translators) seem ponderous and pedestrian, but his translation as a whole is remarkable for its vigorous, rhythmic prose and its consistent lucidity. Luther's Bible had a decisive influence on the evolution of standard German and is the most important single element in the German literary heritage. It was, in a sense, his reparation for the divisive results of his religious revolution. 'It created,' wrote Thomas Mann, 'the modern German language as a vehicle of literary expression and gave literary unity to a country divided in religion and politically dismembered.'

(2)

'Morally subversive, economically destructive, socially degrading, confused in its causes, devious in its course, it is the outstanding example in European history of meaningless conflict.' This is C. V. Wedgwood's view of the Thirty Years War, the last of the wars of religion, in the sense that the opposing factions, Imperialists and Evangelicals, operated behind a screen of religious dogma. It was fought out on German soil in the first half of the seventeenth century and while its impact on the arts was less crippling than might be supposed, it had a powerful and enduring influence on the climate of thought and feeling. The mutability of human affairs, the fickleness of fortune, the yearning for order amid chaos, the need for constancy and fortitude as defences against the flux of life—these are the themes which sound repeatedly in the poetry and prose of the seventeenth century. They are woven into the fabric of the first great novel in the German language—Grimmelshausen's *Der abenteuerliche Simplicissimus* (*The Adventures of Simplicissimus,* 1669).

Much of *Simplicissimus* is based on Grimmelshausen's own experience of the Thirty Years War: he was press-ganged by Hessian mercenaries at the age of ten, and for fourteen years was tossed hither and thither by the tide of war, probably serving now on one side, now on the other. His novel is not easily defined; it is picaresque in form, religious in substance, in part a realistic war-story, in part a topical satire on the rift between Christian ideals and unchristian practice, in part an allegory of the human condition, valid for all time. His hero, in his early days at least, is an innocent astray in a wicked world. Brought up by peasant foster-parents in the highland forests of the Spessart, he takes refuge, when his village is overrun by troops, with a hermit. His wise and world-weary mentor nicknames him 'Simplicius' because his ignorance of the ways of God and man is total, and instils into him a kind of elemental Christianity. With this basic equipment, Simplicius sets out into the world, finding it as strange as it finds him crazy—he begins his confused career as a buffoon in the service of the military governor of Hanau. He is swept into the war and for a time sees it with the clear vision of a child, unclouded by ideological fog, recording its brutality and confusion with wide-eyed wonder. His simplicity soon wears off and he adapts himself to the way of the world. He explores whatever experiences it has to offer, becoming in turn a man-at-arms, a highwayman, and a farmer; he makes two disastrous marriages, wins and loses a fortune, tastes high life in Paris, and penetrates to distant regions, to Russia, Korea, and Japan. The course of his life comes full circle and he ends where he began, in the solitude of the Spessart, devoted to study and contemplation in what seems a secure retreat; but the pull of the world is strong and in the second edition of his novel Grimmelshausen has to translate him to a remoter sanctuary on a desert island.

Simplicissimus is rounded off with an 'Adieu, Welt', a farewell to the world taken word for word from the Spanish moralist Antonio de Guevara. This gloomy tailpiece is out of joint with the rest of the story. Grimmelshausen puts on a decent show of moral indignation and pessimism, but resist it as he may, cheerfulness keeps breaking in; if one side of him is appalled at the vanity of the world, the other is enthralled by its anarchic variety and it is with more relish than disgust that he chronicles the iniquity of his time.

There is no stranger period in German literature than the seventeenth century. No other age is so rich in curiosities of literature; none can show such violent contrasts of mood and such a medley of styles. Epigrammatic terseness and luxuriant verbosity, powerful feelings and intellectual conceits, fervent religiosity and rhetorical bombast, erotic hymns and spiritual love-songs—all these will be found in Baroque poetry. It was the work of amateurs (a profession of letters came into being much later) impelled by a variety of motives; on the one hand we have pastors and priests who wrote for the greater glory of God or to communicate their mystical intimacy with Him; on the other we have academics and administrators using literature both as an avenue of advancement and an escape from painful anxieties and perplexities. A generally sombre view of life went together with a delight in literary experiment, induced by the belated impact of the Renaissance on Germany. Literary societies, on the model of the Italian academies, sprang up under august patronage, devoted to the reform of German poetry and the refinement of the language; there was a copious output of aids to composition, ranging from the *Buch von der deutschen Poeterey* (1624) by Martin Opitz, the most influential German critic of the century, to a manual which proposed to teach the art of German poetics and metrics in six lessons; critical principles derived from France and Holland were applied to German literature, Romance forms like the sonnet were imported, and the French alexandrine became the line most favoured by the poets and dramatists of the time. Their plays, mainly intended for performance in schools and universities, were too suggestive of the literary exercise or too eccentric to make an impression outside Germany and only unrepresentative fragments of their verse have reached us: a handful of hymns by Paul Gerhardt, a few of Friedrich von Logau's 3,000 epigrams translated by Longfellow, among them his forbidding 'Retribution':

> Though the mills of God grind slowly, yet they grind
>   exceeding small;
> Though with patience He stand waiting, with exactness
>   grinds He all.

Logau was one of a group of writers and critics who were either born in, or worked in, Silesia, the chief area of literary activity in seventeenth-century Germany. The most considerable of them was Andreas Gryphius—poet, dramatist, scholar, and functionary: after the end of the war, and after a long period in Holland at the University of Leyden, he became syndic of the principality of Glogau. Although Gryphius has a gloomy reputation—he was a specialist in funeral orations and wrote a series of poems entitled *Kirchhofs-Gedanken* (*Graveyard Thoughts*)—he kept amid his troubled life a sense of the absurd; it found an outlet in his comedies, one of them, *Peter Squenz*, an adaptation of the 'tedious brief scene' of Pyramus and Thisbe in *A Midsummer Night's Dream*. His tragedies are moral allegories, extolling the fortitude of ancient and modern martyrs in face of undeserved suffering, and include a vindication of Charles the First of England entitled *Ermordete Majestät* (*Murdered Majesty*) begun shortly after the execution of the King in 1649. Gryphius is a heavy-handed dramatist, ramming home his message with the help of staccato dialogue and endless monologues. When he works within narrower limits his writing is on an altogether higher level. The sonnet with its close formation and the alexandrine with its measured pace gave him precisely the discipline he needed; in a poem like 'Abend', one of a quartet on the times of day, commonplace enough in theme and imagery, they combine to produce a rare effect of gravity and pathos:

> Der schnelle Tag ist hin, die Nacht schwingt ihre Fahn'
> Und führt die Sternen auf. Der Menschen müde Scharen
> Verlassen Feld und Werk; wo Tier' und Vögel waren,
> Traurt jetzt die Einsamkeit. Wie ist die Zeit vertan!
> Der Port naht mehr und mehr sich zu der Glieder Kahn.
> Gleich wie dies Licht verfiel, so wird in wenig Jahren
> Ich, du, und was man hat, und was man sieht, hinfahren.
> Dies Leben kommt mir vor als eine Rennebahn:
> Laß, höchster Gott, mich doch nicht auf dem Laufplatz
>   gleiten,
> Laß mich nicht Ach, nicht Pracht, nicht Lust, nicht Angst
>   verleiten,
> Dein ewig heller Glanz sei vor und neben mir,
> Laß, wenn der müde Leib entschläft, die Seele wachen,
> Und wenn der letzte Tag wird mit mir Abend machen,
> So reiß mich aus dem Tal der Finsternis zu dir!

The religious poetry of Gryphius is in the nature of common prayer; it voices shared anxieties and general tribulations. A more intimate variety of religious experience is transmitted in *Der Cherubinische Wandersmann* (*The Cherubic Wanderer*, 1675) by Angelus Silesius, the pen-name of Johann Scheffler. His poetry is in the main an exposition of traditional mystical doctrine, offering guidance on the conduct of the inner life and depicting the intercourse of the soul with God. Unoriginal in content, it is exceptionally precise in form. Silesian mysticism had a cloudy source, the writings of Jakob Böhme, but there is nothing unclear about Scheffler's epigrammatic couplets; he is the most lucid and economical of metaphysical poets. He can make one metaphor do the work of twenty:

> Nichts ist, das dich bewegt, du selber bist das Rad,
> Das aus sich selbsten lauft, und keine Ruhe hat.

He can give sharp definition to such philosophical abstractions as 'accident and essence':

> Mensch, werde wesentlich; denn wenn die Welt vergeht,
> So fällt der Zufall weg, das Wesen, das besteht.

In the lines 'Gott lebt nicht ohne mich' he takes up a theme, the dependence of God upon man, of which a lesser poet might have made pretentious nonsense. Angelus Silesius handles it with a light touch and produces a singular effect, somewhere between innocence and arrogance:

> Ich weiß, daß ohne mich Gott nicht ein Nu kann leben;
> Werd ich zunicht, er muß von Not den Geist aufgeben.

Such disarming simplicity is rare in German Baroque poetry.

3

The Eighteenth Century

(1)

MOST literatures have their golden age, at least in the imagination of
later generations looking back from present mediocrity to bygone
glory. German literature has no equivalent of the Elizabethan age or
the age of Louis XIV but in its history the eighteenth century was a
significant turning-point. At its outset, German men of letters were
thin on the ground and of no consequence abroad. At its close, the
prestige of German literature was high; amid a multitude of
scriveners, we find a cluster of outstanding minds, who have become
classics in the sense that they set the standards by which Germans
have ever since judged their writers. It is an awkward period for the
literary historian. For one thing, it is overshadowed by Goethe, who
straddles the eighteenth and the nineteenth centuries: he was born
shortly after the death of Pope and died not long before the birth of
Thomas Hardy. For another, the impression we get of the period
from the non-literary arts, from late Baroque and Rococo architecture, from the music of Bach, Haydn, and Mozart, is at odds with the
experience of the writers who lived through it. Towards its end,
Goethe wrote an essay entitled *Literarischer Sansculottismus* (*Literary Mobocracy*) in which he defended his fellow writers against the
attacks of a Berlin critic: given the conditions under which they lived
and worked, their successes were as admirable as their failures were
understandable; they lacked the stimulating environment of a
capital city like Paris or London; they were confused by a tasteless

public incapable of discriminating between the good and the second-rate; they were hindered rather than helped by an aristocracy whose cultural values were imported from France. The root of the trouble, in Goethe's view, was the fragmentation of German culture in his day. Until Napoleon reshaped it early in the nineteenth century, 'Germany' was a conglomeration of several hundred states, ecclesiastical principalities, and free cities, 'Austria' the nucleus of the vast multi-racial Habsburg empire. This singular political configuration and the underlying social structure affected the arts in various ways. Architecture and music, notably opera, flourished under the patronage of the courts and the Church, however much Mozart and others like him might suffer from their patrons. Although men like Lessing, Herder, Schiller, and Goethe were all sustained by some form of direct or indirect patronage, literature came off worse, for its German practitioners had small prestige value. When Frederick the Great, whose language was French and whose favourite author was Racine, wished to attract a great man of letters to the Prussian court, he picked on Voltaire. Not that he was indifferent to German literature: he wrote an essay on it, *De la littérature allemande*, pointing out its shortcomings, the reasons for them and the means by which they could be corrected. Uncouth though they might be, German writers were not without promise and would eventually, once they had been licked into shape by a course of classical discipline, take their place as peers among European men of letters.

Goethe, on the other hand, believed that Germany could not be expected to throw up 'classical' writers as he understood the term—members of a closely knit and congenial community whose thoughts and feelings they shared and expressed. Born into isolation, subjected to radically different kinds of education, buoyed up by no national tradition, they were thrown back upon themselves and forced to make capital of their idiosyncrasies. For Mme de Staël, surveying German culture a little later in *De l'Allemagne*, these apparent handicaps were a positive advantage. She had, of course, an axe to grind; she wrote *De l'Allemagne* as much to reprove France as to illuminate Germany and praises the spiritualism of Germany—'la patrie de la pensée'—the better to castigate French materialism. Admittedly, her task was complicated by the dearth of common ideas and the abundance of original ideas in Germany and by the contrasts she encountered. Exuberant imagination was coupled with what she called 'cette éminente faculté de penser qui s'élève et se perd dans le vague'; a union of civilization and nature had not yet been achieved. Nevertheless, she extolled Germany as a land of poets and thinkers, high-minded and industrious solitaries, indifferent to good form and the social arts, disinterested seekers after truth.

'Tatenarm und gedankenvoll'—poor in deeds and rich in thought: this was how Friedrich Hölderlin described his countrymen in his ode 'An die Deutschen'. He might have added 'rich in feeling', for there was as much sensibility as sense in the temper of his age. In the second half of the century, notably during the period of 'Storm and Stress', a powerful current of feeling broke through, whereas in the first half we find an abundance of writing reflecting upon life rather than bodying it forth. Much of it was inspired by the ideas and ideals of the Enlightenment, which was marked in Germany by the close association of philosophy and theology. The mathematician and philosopher Gottfried Wilhelm Leibniz, for example, found time amid his more abstract labours to write for the benefit of the Queen of Prussia, who was troubled by religious doubts, a *Theodicy*, in which he discoursed on such matters as the goodness of God, the freedom of Man, and the origin of Evil. When Immanuel Kant, later in the century, attempted to define the nebulous term 'Enlightenment' he did so with an eye to the religious temper of the age; less concerned than Leibniz to reconcile reason and faith, he defined Enlightenment as 'the emergence of man from his self-imposed tutelage', meaning that enslavement by irrational dogma for which man had only his own laziness and cowardice to blame. The conviction that reason, once liberated, could solve all problems was as widespread as the conviction that it is our destiny to develop, by dint of such agencies as education and art, in the direction of perfect humanity; believers and unbelievers alike were animated by their faith in an orderly, intelligible, and meaningful world. Given this climate of thought, it is not surprising that we encounter throughout the period many attempts, at varying levels of sophistication, to

assert eternal Providence
and justify the ways of God to Men.

At one extreme we have Goethe's *Faust*; at the other we have a poem
like Christian Fürchtegott Gellert's 'Die Ehre Gottes aus der Natur'
('God's Majesty divined in Nature'), which has achieved immortality
of a kind in Beethoven's setting of the first two verses. Gellert bids us
behold the wonders of Nature, as a manifestation of the divine
attributes of wisdom, order and power. Such is his intimacy with the
Deity that he can, with no sense of incongruity, assume His voice
and use Him, in the finale of the poem, to confirm his personal
estimate of His nature:

> Ich bin dein Schöpfer, bin Weisheit und Güte,
> Ein Gott der Ordnung und dein Heil;
> Ich bins! Mich liebe von ganzem Gemüte,
> Und nimm an meiner Gnade teil.

Gellert was a poet-pedagogue, Professor of Philosophy and Ethics
at the University of Leipzig, and in the judgement of Frederick the
Great 'le plus raisonnable de tous savants allemands'. Goethe, who
attended his lectures on poetics in the 1760s, found him a popular, if
lugubrious and excessively earnest teacher and recalled, in his auto-
biography, the care with which Gellert corrected the essays he sub-
mitted to him, adding where necessary observations of a moral
nature, for Goethe's imaginative prose was little to his rationalist
taste. His *Geistliche Oden und Lieder* (*Spiritual Odes and Songs,*
1757) and his well-turned verse fables were widely read and so
highly esteemed that Goethe describes them as the basis of German
moral culture in the mid-eighteenth century. Gellert's aim, he tells
us, was to impart the truth, by means of pictures, to those of little
intellectual capacity. His kind of poetry, dispassionate and cerebral as
befitted his practical view of the poet's function, gave way in the
latter half of the period to the exuberant and heartfelt variety practised by writers like Friedrich Gottlieb Klopstock.

Klopstock's spiritual songs and odes are a far cry from Gellert's.
Whereas Gellert is down to earth, Klopstock rarely touches ground;
he is for ever soaring into the infinite, borne aloft by a current of
rapturous enthusiasm. The Deity he addresses in his ode 'An Gott' is

no remote principle of order and wisdom, but an indwelling presence which speaks to us through our feelings:

> Ein stiller Schauer deiner Allgegenwart
> Erschüttert, Gott! mich. Sanfter erbebt mein Herz
> Und mein Gebein. Ich fühl', ich fühl' es,
> Daß du auch hier, wo ich weine, Gott! bist.

Herder, a critic who judged literature by the strength of its emotional impact, credited him with the creation of a new poetic language; Klopstock, he said, gave 'a voice to our heart'. His experiments with free rhythms and classical metres, his novel sentence structures and emotive diction are all directed to one end—the excitement of powerful, indeterminate feelings. His major work was a gigantic religious epic in hexameters, *Der Messias* (*The Messiah*, 1748–73). The model was Milton, but *The Messiah* lacks the sinew of *Paradise Lost* and *Paradise Regained*; it is all spirit and no body, an exercise in the expression of the ineffable; the substance, Christ's passion, is obscured by a haze of sentiment. No clear line can be drawn between Klopstock's religious and secular verse; even when he is dealing with nature, friendship, or love he strikes a note of fervent piety. The persistent strain of religiosity in his work has its roots in the religious revival in the Lutheran Church, originating in the seventeenth century, to which its opponents, with intent to ridicule it, gave the name of Pietism. Few major writers of the period escaped the influence of the movement. Some, like Lessing and Wieland, were brought up in Pietist parsonages, some, like Schiller and Herder, in Pietist households, others, like Goethe, felt its impact during their formative years. It affected literature less through its doctrine, which was set out by Philipp Jakob Spener in his *Pia Desideria oder herzliches Verlangen nach gottgefälliger Besserung der wahren evangelischen Kirche* (*Heartfelt Desires for the Reform, pleasing to God, of the True Evangelical Church*) than through the kind of sensibility it bred in its adherents. In reaction against Lutheran orthodoxy, the Pietists developed a highly emotional form of worship, indulged in agonies of repentance and ecstasies of rebirth, cultivated habits of intense self-scrutiny, and kept a vigilant eye on the spiritual state of their children.

The concern of both Pietists and rationalists with the inner man left as clear a mark on prose as on poetry; the novelists of the period tell us much about their thoughts and feelings, little about the world in which they lived. One of them, Johann Paul Friedrich Richter, who used the pen-name Jean Paul, was beloved in Germany and admired abroad by writers like Carlyle and De Quincey as a chronicler of rural life, but his country parsons and village school-masters and their idyllic surroundings now seemed bathed in a glow of improbable mellowness. His more ambitious works, such as *Titan* (1800–3) and *Flegeljahre* (*Years of Indiscretion*, 1804–5), match Goethe's definition of the novel as a subjective epic, in which the writer begs leave to handle the world in his own way. 'The only question is,' Goethe added, 'if he has a way or not; the rest will take care of itself.' Jean Paul took the way of eccentricity; he wrote chiefly about himself, his idiosyncrasies, the rift in his personality between the enthusiast and the realist, and ballasted his stories with ponderous humour, decking them with luxuriant metaphors and allusions to the miscellaneous information stored in his mind. He had a marked pedagogic streak and wrote a highly regarded treatise on education, *Levana*, which reflects the positive obsession of the age with the schooling of the personality, with 'Bildung'.

(2)

It was in the latter half of the eighteenth century that the 'Bil-dungsroman', Germany's chief contribution to the art of the novel, took shape. The 'Bildungsroman', of which Goethe's *Wilhelm Meister* is a classic example, traces the growth of a personality towards some form of mental, moral, and emotional maturity deter-mined by the writer's view of life. There is little attempt to give an illusion of life and little action: the plot is a device for expediting the hero's progress from one stage of development to the next, the characters are symbols of the influences which shape his personality. One such novel is *Die Geschichte des Agathon* (*The Story of Agathon*, 1767) by Christoph Martin Wieland. Wieland, author of satirical and philosophical novels and verse romances, editor of many years of the influential periodical *Der deutsche Merkur* and translator of Shakespeare, spent the latter part of his life in Weimar, summoned there by the Duchess Anna Amalie as tutor to her sons, the elder of them being Goethe's later patron Karl August. Traces of an earlier period as Professor of Philosophy at the University of Erfurt are apparent in *Agathon*, in which the philosopher has the upper hand of the story-teller. It took nearly thirty years to finish and is a record of Wieland's own progress, as he saw it, from the Pietist 'Schwärmerei' of his youth to the urbane rationalism of his middle age, written to help us fit ourselves 'for a world in which rational beings, governed by conscience, inspired by justice and wisdom, strive in harmony for perfection'. The setting, ancient Greece in the heyday of Greek thought, serves as camouflage for Wieland's Germany and the intellectual forces at work in it. Agathon, brought up on Orphic mysteries in a secluded Delphic temple, goes out into the world a Platonic idealist and finds, with the help of the Sophists and Pythagoreans he encounters, a middle way between materialism and idealism, scepticism and credulity. Wieland claimed a measure of realism for his novel and is not indifferent to the emotions—Agathon's educators include the beautiful prostitute Danae—but his real interest is in his hero's intellect. His *Agathon* is an analysis of the development of a personality through intercourse with other minds rather than through action and experience.

For a clearer impression of life in eighteenth-century Germany and Switzerland, we must turn to autobiographies like Goethe's *Dichtung und Wahrheit* (*Poetry and Truth*) and the *Lebensgeschichte und natürliche Abenteuer des armen Mannes in Toggenburg* (*Life Story and Adventures of the Poor Man of Toggenburg*) by the Swiss Ulrich Bräker, or to autobiographical novels like Karl Philipp Moritz's *Anton Reiser* (1785–90). *Anton Reiser* is something of a landmark in European fiction. Moritz gave it the sub-title 'a psychological novel' and described it as an attempt to present, as exactly as possible, a human life down to its smallest details. It is an account of the first twenty years of his own life, coloured by unhappy memories of his youth but substantially true, an acute analysis of the degree to which a personality can be made or marred by the apparently trivial circumstances and emotional disturbances of childhood and adolescence. It gives moreover a vivid picture of life in an artisan community, in school and university, and throws light upon such features of the 'Storm and Stress' generation as their theatre mania and delusions of genius. Moritz has been called the seismograph of his age; he exhibits in an extreme form the stresses and strains to which his generation was subject. Goethe, who befriended him when he was in Italy, had a high regard for him and thought of him as a kind of younger brother, victim of a harsher fate than his own. In his short life—he died in 1793 at the age of thirty-six—Moritz produced a miscellany of works on prosody, mythology, and aesthetics and an account of his travels in England (*Reisen eines Deutschen in England im Jahre 1782*). He was a teacher with a strong interest in child psychology, a schoolmaster, and later professor of aesthetics and the study of classical antiquity at the Berlin Academy of Fine Arts, founder and editor of the *Magazin für Erfahrungsseelenkunde* (*Journal of Empirical Psychology*), for which *Anton Reiser* was originally intended. Although it was meant to help teachers to a better understanding of their pupils, it is not an educational novel like Rousseau's *Émile* or Pestalozzi's *Gertrud*; far from prescribing some ideal system of education, Moritz, concerned to get to the roots of his own tensions and contradictions, exposes the dire effects of a loveless home, misguided indoctrination, and the humiliations of poverty on a tender human organism.

Anton, whose parents were members of a Quietist sect devoted to the mortification of the passions and individuality, grows up incapable of distinguishing clearly between the real and the imaginary or of keeping a balance between self-denigration and self-dramatization. He becomes stage-struck while still at school, finding in the fantasy world of the theatre an outlet for suppressed emotion, a vantage-point from which he could exercise control over men's minds and feelings, and thus win the instant applause for which he hungered. The novel ends with an account of his frustrated efforts to join one of the theatrical companies touring Germany at the time. It is written in an unadorned, documentary style, enlivened by Moritz's sense of the absurd and the unobtrusive irony with which he writes of this hero's literary diet and ambitions. After his father had taught him to read with the help of a spelling-book and a treatise against spelling, Anton graduated to the Bible and the lives of the saints and was exposed in adolescence to the full rigours of the age of sentiment. He owed the dreariest hours of his life to his friend, the theological student Neries, who read to him the whole of Klopstock's *Messias*; whereas Neries had the advantage of reading aloud, Anton was compelled to listen and express delight, guilt-ridden at his inability to respond to the lofty poetry ringing in his ears. He himself begins a poem on the Creation and never gets beyond an attempt to depict original Chaos; vast images and conceptions loom up in his mind, but all his tongue produces are stammering sounds something like those in Klopstock's odes. Moritz writes perceptively of the preference of poets without true creative power for lofty themes, rather than those close to men: 'to everyday subjects their genius must impart the elevation which in uncommon topics they hope to find ready-made'.

We can see in *Anton Reiser* a reaction, given practical form in the work of educationalists like Pestalozzi and Froebel, against the prevailing attitude to the child. As an illustration of this we have a revealing portrait of the critic and dramatist Gotthold Ephraim Lessing and his brother Theophilus, painted when they were aged about seven or eight. On the right sits Gotthold in knee breeches and wig, an open book on his knee, a pile of books at his side; on the left Theophilus with shaven head, dressed in clerical black, offering an ear of corn to a lamb—two sedate and miniature adults, reflecting a view of infancy as a regrettable interlude between birth and rational manhood.

(3)

According to Pushkin, it was only in German literature that the critics came before the authors. However dubious the generalization, it is a reminder of the strong influence which Lessing, Herder, and figures on the literary fringe like the art historian Johann Winckelmann had on their contemporaries. Lessing was, of course, a dramatist with a significant place in German theatrical history, but his three major plays, his tragedy *Emilia Galotti*, his comedy *Minna von Barnhelm*, and his dramatic poem *Nathan der Weise* were by-products of either his critical or ideological concerns. He was unable to discover in himself, as he readily admitted, much evidence of original genius.

In his twenties, Lessing earned a precarious living as a literary journalist in Berlin—he was one of the first freelances in German literature—and served an uneasy apprenticeship to Voltaire, at that time resident celebrity at Frederick the Great's court. He was for five years secretary to the Prussian governor of Breslau, acted for a short time as literary adviser to the Hamburg National Theatre, and ended as court librarian to the Duke of Brunswick. He died in 1781. He was constantly under pressure, from the demands of his journalism, from the theological controversies in which he involved himself, and from his many interests: he spread his talent over various fields, including classical philology, archaeology, and aesthetics. His criticism, scattered in periodicals or in fragmentary works like his *Hamburgische Dramaturgie*, is concentrated upon drama, which was for him the corner-stone of the arts. His most systematic treatise (which never got beyond the first part) had, however, nothing to do with drama. Entitled *Laokoon oder Über die Grenzen der Malerei und Poesie* (*Laokoon or On the Boundaries between Painting and Poetry*, 1766), it was an attempt to assign to the literary and visual arts their proper province and is characteristic of his method. Instead of reflecting in abstract fashion upon Art, he prefers to tackle such concrete problems as come his way and is at his best when making illuminating distinctions or clearing away the debris left by previous critics.

Lessing embodied the most amiable features of the Enlightenment. He was admired, even by the Romantics, as much for his quality as for his substance, for his lucid style, his hardy personality, at once combative and tolerant, and his honesty of mind. He was the least arrogant of rationalists, preferring the pursuit to the monopoly of truth. A year before his death he wrote his testament, *Die Erziehung des Menschengeschlechts* (*The Education of the Human Race*, 1780), a series of bold assertions alternating with wistful questions, based on the proposition: 'What education is to the individual, so is revelation to the whole of mankind.' It begins drily enough as a treatise on revealed religion and ends with a vision of human destiny as a progress towards total enlightenment and purity, towards an age of perfection in which men will do good without hope of reward in this world or the next. We are in the hands of a great Preceptor who observes order and measure in all things and reveals to us no more of the truth than befits the stages of our evolution. His methods may be devious but that they are purposeful is plain to all reasonable men: 'Was erzogen wird, wird zu Etwas erzogen'—what is educated is educated to some specific end. The process is slow and life is short, but Lessing does not despair, for he sees a hope of immortality in the doctrine of the transmigration of souls. What cannot be accomplished in one existence can be accomplished in successive reincarnations. Why then, asks Lessing, should I be impatient? Is not all eternity mine?

Lessing was a moralist, and never more so than in his handling of drama. He joined in the never-ending debate about the nature and function of tragedy, using learned arguments which all tend in the same direction—to the view that tragedy is a school of morals. Its business is to improve us by stirring our emotions in a special way, and to reassure us by mirroring in its construction and probability the order and measure of the world. The more plausible the action of a tragedy, the more readily can we identify ourselves with the characters, share in their sufferings and experience the basic tragic emotion: pity. The belief that tragedy, before it can achieve anything else, must move us lies at the root of Lessing's hostility to the French classical dramatists and his admiration for Shakespeare, a dramatist he thought much more in line with the robust taste of the German public than Corneille or Voltaire. In Lessing's day, changes were afoot in the German stage; the towns were replacing the courts as centres of theatrical activity, the strolling players of the seventeenth and early-eighteenth centuries were settling down in municipal repertory theatres on the model of the Hamburg National Theatre, a new public was emerging, demanding entertainment within the range of its own experience, reflecting its own problems and ideals. Lessing's response to these changes was to champion English as opposed to French models and to naturalize in Germany the tragedy of common life with its heroes and heroines of the middling sort, neither monsters nor martyrs, designed to move us to sympathetic grief rather than anger at injustice or terror at inscrutable fate.

As a dramatist, Lessing began with comedies in the Molière vein and wrote his first tragedy, *Miss Sara Sampson*, in 1752. It owed much to George Lillo's *The Merchant of London* and to Richardson's novel *Pamela or Virtue Rewarded*, was the first German domestic tragedy, but was otherwise undistinguished. *Emilia Galotti*, written twenty years later, served Lessing's successors as a model of dramatic construction and was admired by Goethe as more up to date than his own early work. It is an ingenious piece of dramatic geometry, based on the Roman legend of Virginia, the plebeian girl killed by her father to save her from dishonour at the hands of the decemvir Appius Claudius. In Lessing's version of the story, set in a small Italian court, Emilia, under heavy temptation to become the mistress of the Prince of Guastalla, induces her father, Odoardo Galotti, a professional soldier with a rugged sense of honour, to kill her. The finale of the play, her death, is in a sense Lessing's starting point; he works back from it, trying to motivate it fully and manoeuvre Emilia and Odoardo into an insoluble but plausible dilemma. So that the spectator's pity shall be unconfined, he gives chance and human frailty an equal share in the murder, for which all the characters are responsible but of which none, apart from the Prince's villainous chamberlain Marinelli, is guilty.

Minna von Barnhelm (1767), the first German play ever performed in England (at the Haymarket in 1786) got short shrift from George Meredith in his *Essay on Comedy*. 'Lessing,' he wrote, 'tried his hand at comedy, with sobering effect upon his readers. The intention to produce the reverse effect is just visible and therein ... consists the fun.' Meredith is less than fair. *Minna von Barnhelm* set the fashion for 'ernste Komödien', problematic comedies, which is still current in the German theatre but its value is more than historical. It is a well-turned and entertaining piece, in which Lessing tried to steer a course between the farces and sentimental comedies of his time. His aim was what he called 'true comedy', designed to move us to laughter and tears and train us to spot the ridiculous, even when it wears the mask of virtue. Old and new elements are blended in the play. The situation—a pair of estranged lovers united after surmounting a series of intricate obstacles—is as old as the art of comedy, the minor characters are stock types. The hero, Major von Tellheim, and Minna the heroine were, however, drawn from contemporary life, and the setting—Berlin shortly after the end of the Seven Years War —was modern. Tellheim is a Prussian officer, crippled, impoverished, and unjustly cashiered, whose over-developed sense of honour leads him to break off his engagement to Minna, a Saxon heiress. His trouble is not a moral flaw, still less a vice; it is an excess of virtue, and he is cured of this admirable if ridiculous failing by the good sense and guile of Minna. If the play has its sombre scenes, there is a generous supply of happy endings: we are promised a double marriage, between Tellheim and Minna and between their servants, Tellheim's good name is restored and the balance of nature is redressed.

Towards the end of his life, Lessing ran foul of the Lutheran Church and having been forbidden to engage directly in theological dispute, turned, as he said, to his old pulpit, the theatre, and wrote *Nathan the Wise* (1779). It is a parable play, written in the blank verse which became the medium of German classical drama, and set in Jerusalem at the time of the Third Crusade. Through the mouth of the Jewish merchant Nathan Lessing preaches his gospel of the brotherhood of man, his belief in right conduct as the gauge of true religion, and in absolute freedom of mind and conscience. 'Kein Mensch muß müssen': in these few words of reproof, addressed to Saladin's treasurer, the Dervish Al-Hafi, Nathan compresses the substance of Lessing's faith.

(4)

'When the heart flies out before the understanding, it saves the judgement a world of pains.' The dictum is Sterne's but it might well have come from Johann Gottfried Herder, the dominating personality in the movement now known as the German Sturm und Drang (Storm and Stress). By profession a churchman and theologian, by inclination a philosopher of history, Herder was a generator of new ideas and a synthesizer on a grand scale of the ideas of others, a pioneer in linguistics, in the historical treatment of world literature, in the cult of folk poetry, and one of the main agents of the revolution in poetics which marked the end of the eighteenth century. The description 'critic' as the term was understood in

Lessing's day fits him awkwardly. He had no patience with the attitude to literature expressed in Pope's maxim:

> Learn hence for ancient rules a just esteem.
> To copy Nature is to copy them.

It was not his way to judge a work by fixed standards of taste or craftsmanship. The whole notion of 'rules' was abhorrent to him, as was the view of the poet as a superior kind of copyist. His view of 'Nature', moreover, differed radically from that of his predecessors. He saw mankind, the nations in which it is organized, the languages and literatures in which they express themselves, in a process of evolution which made nonsense of absolute standards of judgement. He valued literature by the degree of genius or creative energy it displayed and thought it a critic's first duty to identify himself with the writer, read him in the spirit in which he wrote, and judge him by the light of the conditions which produced him. He set little store by sober objectivity or reasoned argument and his style is the reverse of Lessing's—enthusiastic, full of ejaculations, metaphors, and leaps of thought. He despised 'Systemschreiber', systematizers, and his criticism is scattered over a vast range of writings, including some, like his major work, the *Ideen zur Philosophie der Geschichte* (1784–91), which have no direct bearing on literature. He was at his best in his twenties and early thirties, when he wrote his *Fragmente über die neuere deutsche Literatur* (*Fragments on Modern German Literature*, 1766–7), his essay *Von Ähnlichkeit der mittleren englischen und deutschen Dichtkunst* (*On the Similarity of English and German Medieval Poetry*), and the essays on Shakespeare and on folk-poetry he contributed to *Von deutscher Art und Kunst* (*On German Character and Art*), a miscellany, published in 1773, in which he collaborated with Goethe and the historian Justus Möser.

Herder's literary likes and dislikes were coloured by his temperament and upbringing. He came from a Pietist home in East Prussia, the son of an ex-weaver who became an elementary schoolmaster and sacristan. He was a self-made man, never forgot it, and nourished throughout his life a sense of social grievance. At the age of thirty-two he was called to Weimar, at Goethe's suggestion, as general superintendent of clergy, spent the rest of his life there but was ill at ease in his milieu. His duties were irksome without giving him an outlet for his driving ambition. Touchy, aggressive, and mordant of speech, he disapproved of the frivolity of Rococo culture, the abundance of social, and the dearth of moral, conventions at the Weimar court. He was full of zeal but short of charity; with eight children of his own, he begrudged Goethe his one, illegitimate son. His favourite author was Swift, because of Swift's activism, his readiness to put his talent at the service of a cause; his favourite art was music because of the direct and forceful impact it made upon the emotions. He gives the impression of judging the literature of his day by the standard of the Old Testament, finding it, in comparison with the Song of Songs and the Book of Job somewhat less than full-blooded, too abstract, genteel, and dispassionate. It was in folk poetry that he found the virtues lacking in modern literature. Whereas Bishop Percy, in his preface to the *Reliques of Ancient English Poetry*, had been apologetic—his aim, he said, was to show 'by what gradations barbarity was civilized, grossness refined and ignorance instructed', Herder in his essay on *Ossian and the Songs of Ancient Peoples* holds up primitive song as a model for the modern poet. His defence of folk-poetry is based on a view of poetic diction which anticipates Wordsworth's preface to the *Lyrical Ballads* by nearly thirty years. Undistracted by shadowy abstractions and what Herder calls 'half ideas', still less by affectation, slavish expectations of preferment, and ignoble political considerations, the folk poet was able to match his thoughts and feelings to his words and achieve a direct relation between the two. In his own over-civilized age, Herder found vestiges of this old and natural speech only among children, women, and those whose minds had been shaped more by practical activity than by speculation. His own speculations, based insecurely on his enthusiasm for Ossian, were less important than his activity as a collector of international folk-poetry. The anthology of *Volkslieder* which he published in the 1770s was the first of its kind, introduced the term 'folk-song' into the literary vocabulary and helped to establish this kind of poetry as the norm of the German lyric.

Herder's Shakespeare essay in *Von deutscher Art und Kunst* was an episode in the battle of the ancients and moderns fought out in

Germany in the latter part of the eighteenth century. For one party, Shakespeare was a natural genius, beyond the reach of dramatic conventions; for the other, he was a tasteless barbarian, ignorant of the rules—a view which becomes more intelligible if we realize on what imperfect knowledge of Shakespeare it was based. Many Germans knew their Shakespeare through Wieland's prose translation, which uncovered the bare bones of the plays but totally obscured the poetry in which they were clothed. For example, Juliet's lines:

> O be some other name!
> What's in a name? that which we call a rose
> By any other name would smell as sweet

comes through in Wieland's version as: 'Was ist ein Name? Das Ding, das wir eine Rose nennen, würde unter jedem andern Namen eben so lieblich riechen.' Herder attacked the practice of judging Shakespeare by the standards of a bygone age; the confusion of his plays was, he argued, an expression of the complexity of Elizabethan life and was in any case, only apparent: Shakespeare, through force of genius and verbal magic, created a universe of his own, a timeless and spaceless dream world to which conventional notions of probability and dramatic unity cannot be applied, but for all that coherent, and uniquely soul-stirring.

'Der tollgewordene Shakespeare', Shakespeare gone mad—this was the nickname given to Friedrich Maximilian Klinger, whose play *Sturm und Drang* (1776) provided a label for the group of young writers associated with Goethe in the 1770s. Their favourite medium was drama; it gave them a congenial outlet for their fantasies and conflicts and offered them the illusory hope, for their plays were rarely performed, of making a direct and powerful impact on the public. Disregarding logic, they rebelled against the use of French models for German drama and, instead, sought originality by imitating Shakespeare, who was for them a symbol of unfettered genius riding roughshod over the niceties of classical form. As Goethe wrote at the time: 'Better a confused play than a cold one.' Klinger seems to have written *Sturm und Drang*, which originally had the apt title *Der Wirrwarr* (*The Hurly-Burly*) according to this prescription. The action is based on a feud between two noble British families, the Bushys and the Berkeleys, and takes place in America, whither they have been banished. It ends tamely enough with a reconciliation and the element of storm and stress is embodied in Lord Bushy's son, Karl, who makes his way to America, via Russia and Spain, under the name of Wild, accompanied by his friends, the eccentric La Feu and the world-weary Blasius. Consumed by an inner fire of discontent, bursting with superfluous health and energy, he seeks death in battle and hopes to find it in the War of Independence. War, he tells us, is his only joy, but he ends by finding happiness in the arms of the sweetheart of his youth, Lord Berkeley's daughter Karoline. Klinger himself, after a brief spell in the theatre, entered military service, became a lieutenant-general in the Russian army, and married an illegitimate daughter of Catherine the Great—an example of the way in which time, as a Soviet ambassador to Great Britain once observed, takes care of all angry young men.

Time dealt less kindly with Jakob Michael Reinhold Lenz, who was next to Goethe the most gifted of the Sturm und Drang writers. Insanity, followed by a dismal end in Moscow, was his lot. He seemed to Goethe like a meteor which flashed over the horizon of German literature and then disappeared without trace, but he was not, in fact, forgotten. Georg Büchner wrote a perceptive and sympathetic account of his mental breakdown and towards the end of the nineteenth century he was resurrected as a pioneer of realism in the theatre. In plays like *Die Soldaten* (*The Soldiers*, 1776) and *Der Hofmeister oder Vorteile der Privaterziehung* (*The Tutor or The Advantages of Private Education*, 1774) he mixes tragedy and comedy, grotesque caricature and sharp observation of social types, in an effort to recapture the reality, and the variety, of the world as he saw it. His *Anmerkungen übers Theater* (*Observations on the Theatre*, 1774) contain, amid much arid theorizing, original insights into the nature of drama and a vigorous plea for the total liberty of the writer. The impression he leaves is of unusual talent, disabled by his unbalanced temperament, undeveloped technique, and lack of contact with the living theatre. The other Storm and Stress dramatists, apart from Goethe and Schiller, who wrote his first play when the movement was all but extinct, seem to have strayed into literature because the practical outlets open to their contemporaries in France and England were denied to them. Under pressure from a social structure of exceptional rigidity, they vented their energies in plays about fratricide and parricide, about corruption in high places and the thwarting of true love by class prejudice or political intrigue, projecting their ideal of the 'Kraftgenie', the powerful and ruthless personality, upon their heroes and villains.

Storm and Stress has been described as a revolution in values, as one of those 'radical new starts' which recur in German literature, a movement prefiguring much that we encounter in the Romantic and realist writers of a later age. To judge it by its substance rather than its effects is to perceive what a significant part Herder and Goethe played in it. Their relationship, marked by alternate periods of intimacy and alienation, began in 1770 at Strassburg where Goethe was a student. Herder, five years his senior, served him as mentor and unsparing critic, stimulus, and irritant, and helped him to weather his personal phase of storm and stress. The turbulence of spirit fashionable at the time was for Goethe a painful reality; his unstable temperament and fluid personality stiffened slowly, if ever, into rigid character. But he had two great assets: a hardy talent and an aptitude for creating order out of emotional chaos and unstable thought. It has been said of him that even the incoherences of his youth had their own kind of exactitude. He was able from the start to find the right vehicles for his feelings and ideas. Conflicting moods of rebellion against divine authority and pantheistic yearning for God are clarified and transmitted in early poems like 'Prometheus' and 'Ganymed' through symbols drawn from Greek myth. He embodied both the vulnerable side of his own nature and the frustrated idealism of his generation in Werther, the hero of his first novel and a key figure in European literature. *Die Leiden des jungen Werthers* (*The Sorrows of Young Werther*, 1774) was, and by intent, a shocking book. Its rudiment was a contemporary case of suicide and it ends with a suicide, for which unsatisfied love was but one among many motives. Werther's self-destruction was a protest against the comfortable certainties of Christian and Rationalist orthodoxy, an affirmation that there are questions to which there is no answer, that we are beset by uncontrollable forces and that innocence is no safeguard against malevolent circumstance. A year after *Werther* appeared, Goethe wrote the first draft of his *Faust*. It reflected a literary fashion—others, like Klinger, had dabbled with Faust as a symbol of titanic aspiration—but went far beyond it; fragmentary though it is, it reveals a depth of feeling and a breadth of intellect which puts Goethe in a class apart from his Storm and Stress companions.

(5)

Goethe is nowadays regarded with suspicion. His greatness is not, of course, denied: it is the cause of the trouble. There is in him that quality of nimiety, too-muchness, which Coleridge found displeasing in the Germans. His writings are of daunting bulk and diversity. He is the national poet of a most industrious people and the quantity of information about him is correspondingly enormous; we have numberless critical and biographical studies of him; we have the record of his conversations with not one but several Boswells, to which must be added his own autobiographical writings and diaries and the many volumes of his letters—1,800 of them to Frau von Stein alone. Never in the history of literature has so much been known about a writer's life and personality. Because of his long productive life—he wrote his first plays and poetry before he was twenty and finished *Faust* in the year of his death at the age of eighty-two—and the close correspondence between his life and his work, he has become the exemplar of the flowering of a creative personality. To his devotees he has become a specimen of humanity extended to its fullest dimensions, a Germanic guru whose wisdom can be adapted to suit a wide range of creeds and ideologies. In England, he was ill served by his nineteenth-century advocates. Matthew Arnold's description of him as 'by far our greatest modern man' did his reputation more harm than good in a country which does not readily bow down before strange gods. Thomas Carlyle expounded a Goethe cast in his own granite-like image, a grim prophet of the gospel of work and renunciation. The result has been, to quote a *Times* leader on the occasion of the centenary of his birth, that 'when the Englishman remembers Goethe at all, it is as a very hardened, very wise, very prefectorial elder, ravaged by conflicting passions but finally victorious, the Zeus of an almost aggressively cosy South German Olympus'. Although there are many likenesses of him, from David's bust to Thackeray's pencil sketches, his appearance has taken on a typical character, illustrated by the foregoing quotation: the character of his later, Olympian years. As with his physical, so it is with his spiritual likeness. The picture of him as a remote and venerable sage, constructing all too fragile ideas of 'Humanität' and 'Bildung', obscures his quality as a man for all seasons, not least for the season of youth; much of his best work was done in that early phase of his life when he was far from hardened and anything but wise. The view of him, still current, as 'the last of the great universal geniuses' is mainly based on the scientific work which preoccupied him in his middle years, at a time when the isolation of the sciences one from another was not yet complete and all were branches of 'natural philosophy'. Disinterested in the detail as opposed to the implications of abstract philosophical systems or in metaphysical speculation, Goethe found in the natural sciences, in optics, geology, zoology, and above all in botany, the only disciplines which as he said 'lead us on to firm ground'. He is most at home in the field of organic nature; he is absorbed by its ever-changing structures, by the cycle of growth, decay, and resurrection, by the hidden forces which mould its forms and advance its evolution. His scientific researches might be thought a diversion of his energy into inappropriate byways, but they are of a piece with the rest of him. The same kind of vision operated in them as was at work in his poetry; he applied natural standards to all, and not merely to selected aspects of life. 'The boundless productivity of nature,' he wrote, 'leaves no corner of space unfilled. Consider for a moment our own earth: everything we call evil or sad springs from the fact that nature has no room for all that springs into life and is still less able to give it permanence.' The observation reflects his personal experience of the ruthlessness as well as the prodigality of nature, which sacrifices a thousand seeds so that one may live, and if lucky, prosper.

To compress the whole of Goethe into a survey of this kind would be a foolish undertaking, so no more will be attempted than a reference to the environment in which he worked and to a few aspects of his poetry, prose, and drama. Goethe came to Weimar in 1775 at the invitation of the young Duke, Karl August, impelled less by calculation than by chance and the urge to escape from his native Frankfurt. He was then aged twenty-six, an indifferent lawyer but already a literary celebrity, on the strength of his first substantial play, *Götz von Berlichingen mit der eisernen Hand*, (*Götz von Berlichingen with the Iron Hand*) and his novel *Werther*. He stayed in Weimar, a town of 7,000 inhabitants, capital of a Duchy whose population was no greater than that of an English county town, for the rest of his life, which was conducted, apart from a momentous journey to Italy in his late thirties, within the narrowest of limits. He was slow to accept them and found it hard to reconcile himself to the confines of Weimar. The trouble was partly caused by his labours as a Privy Councillor in the Duke's service. At first, when he was chiefly concerned with the mines, forests, and roads of the Duchy, they were multifarious and unexacting; later, when he became head of the Treasury, he had heavier, but none the less petty, responsibilities and after his return from Italy limited himself to cultural activity, such as the directorship of the Court theatre which he took on reluctantly and held for over twenty years. While his practical work forced him to observe the natural world outside him and thus led him towards science, it crippled the poetic part of him; he wrote a fair amount but completed little apart from a few lyrics. He was, moreover, involved in so painful a struggle for emotional balance, sometimes eased and sometimes aggravated by his involvement with Charlotte von Stein, that he remained to the end reticent about this phase of his life. At the end of his first ten years at Weimar he was in a state bordering on despair. His departure for Italy in the autumn of 1786 was an escape into outer lightness from Germanic gloom and the labyrinth of his own mind, as he made plain in one of the *Roman Elegies* he wrote on his return:

O wie fühl' ich in Rom mich so froh! gedenk' ich der Zeiten,
Da mich ein graulicher Tag hinten im Norden umfing,
Trübe der Himmel und schwer auf meine Scheitel sich senkte,

Farb- und gestaltlos die Welt um den Ermatteten lag,
Und ich über mein Ich, des unbefriedigen Geistes
Düstre Wege zu spähn, still in Betrachtung versank.

Goethe spent the better part of two years in Italy, mainly in Rome. His stay there, recorded in his *Italienische Reise* (*Italian Journey*), was a major turning-point in his life. It would be misleading to say that the experience changed him, for he saw in Italy only what he wanted to see and took from it only what he needed. But he acquired, through the impact of the Italian landscape with its wealth of clear-cut forms, through the classical art on which he concentrated his attention, his characteristic, outward-directed habit of vision and Italy bred in him that belief in the primacy of form, in clarity and order, which marks his mature view of literature and art. He had, moreover, a breathing space in which to make up lost ground; he took with him the drafts of what were to be his major plays, finished off *Iphigenie auf Tauris* and *Egmont*, made headway with *Torquato Tasso*, and wrote, in the incongruous surroundings of the Borghese Gardens in Rome the Witches' Kitchen scene in *Faust*.

When he came back to Weimar, Goethe had difficulty for a time in adjusting himself to an environment he had outgrown. In the end he came to terms with Weimar, induced it to come to terms with him and made a virtue of its necessary limitations. As he put it in one of his 'Sprüche':

Draußen zu wenig oder zuviel,
Zu Hause nur ist Maß und Ziel.

In his *Conversations with Goethe*, Johann Peter Eckermann recalls how Goethe, trying to persuade him to settle in Weimar, said to him: 'Where else will you find so much good in so confined a space?' Weimar gave him a secure base in a troubled time for his wide-ranging intellectual operations and suited his relatively austere but comfortable life-style. Together with the neighbouring University of Jena, in its heyday in the 1790's, it gave him a society of cultivated minds, on the whole congenial, but generating enough friction to burnish his faculties. His closest companion in literature was Schiller, who came to Jena as Professor of History in 1789 and later moved to Weimar. Their collaboration, which lasted from 1794, when they came together after a slow *rapprochement*, to Schiller's death in 1805, is recorded in their correspondence, an invaluable source of information about their aspirations and difficulties, their way of writing, and the genesis of some of their major works. By precept and example, through the periodicals they founded, through the Weimar theatre, they fought a campaign against mediocrity, triviality, and disorder, in literature and art. Their 'classicism', based on Greek standards and on principles of discipline and restraint, was a complex affair, but at the heart of it lay a distaste for what Goethe, in a tart comment, called 'Pfuscherei', bungling ineptitude, the source, in his opinion, of the German love of uncertainty in the arts. A loftier form of the same idea reappears in the finale of that summation of Weimar classicism, his sonnet 'Natur und Kunst' (Nature and Art):

> Wer Großes will, muß sich zusammenraffen;
> In der Beschränkung zeigt sich erst der Meister,
> Und das Gesetz nur kann uns Freiheit geben.

Up to the early years of this century, Weimar remained a symbol of the best elements in the German cultural tradition, and a centre of activity in the arts. It was, for example, in its art schools, which Walter Gropius took over in 1919 and renamed the Bauhaus, that the modern movement in architecture began. Unhappy political associations now cling around the name of Weimar, proving for pessimists the futility of the exalted humanism engendered there in the eighteenth century and reminding the more sanguine that ideals are so called because they are unattainable.

Goethe was before all else a poet, of exceptional range, consistency, and endurance; he is rarely below his best and he wrote as freshly in old age as in youth. Some of his finest verse will be found in *West–östlicher Divan* (*West–Eastern Divan*), a cycle of poems arranged in twelve books written in 1814 and 1815 when he was in his mid-sixties. Its title, derived from the *Divan* or 'collection of songs' of the Persian poet Hafiz indicates the chief of its many themes, the exploration of Eastern thought and poetry by a Western mind. Goethe's ability to renew periodically his sources of poetic energy, his skill in combining lightness with authority, warm feeling with cool thinking, are nowhere more evident than in his *Divan*.

So abundant and various is Goethe's poetry that it is dangerous to generalize about it. What distinguishes him from the poets of our own day, according to one view of him, is his special gift for simplicity of utterance, for direct statement, for 'the illumination of the usual'. Many of his best-known poems undoubtedly have these qualities. There are no far-fetched images, no ingenious metaphors, no extraordinary ideas; the poems spring not from fancy but from experiences so ample that they touch our own at many points. The language is close to everyday speech and the tone is often offhand, even when the theme is solemn. Goethe grumbled about the deficiencies of German as a poetic medium, but he made full use of its wealth of ready-made rhymes and rhythms and adapted them to all kinds of metres and stanzas—Germanic, Romance, Classical, and even Persian. Rarely do we have a sense of strain; we are left instead with that impression of uncontrived rightness which nature, rather than art, usually makes upon us. This, coupled with Goethe's way of making poetry out of the most unlikely material, has led to the view that verse-making was for him as effortless as speech. Effortless as his verse may seem, it was far from a spontaneous overflow of feeling and thought. Poems of quintessential 'simplicity' like the two 'Wandrers Nachtlieder' and 'Gefunden' were retouched so as to get the right sequence of image and sound, mood and thought and produce miniature, but perfectly proportioned works of art. His technique is so assured that he can achieve depth and amplitude by the most unpretentious means. His ability to shape and clarify large tracts of experience with a minimum of effort is clear in 'Um Mitternacht,' a 'Lebenslied' written in his old age for which he had a special liking:

> Um Mitternacht ging ich, nicht eben gerne,
> Klein, kleiner Knabe, jenen Kirchhof hin
> Zu Vaters Haus, des Pfarrers; Stern am Sterne,
> Sie leuchteten doch alle gar zu schön;
>   Um Mitternacht.

Wenn ich dann ferner in des Lebens Weite
Zur Liebsten mußte, mußte, weil sie zog,
Gestirn und Nordschein über mir im Streite,
Ich gehend, kommend Seligkeiten sog;
   Um Mitternacht.

Bis dann zuletzt des vollen Mondes Helle
So klar und deutlich mir ins Finstere drang,
Auch der Gedanke willig, sinnig, schnelle
Sich ums Vergangne wie ums Künftige schlang:
   Um Mitternacht.

There is, of course, more to Goethe than plain speaking. His poetry is often formed out of thoughts that are far from simple or even out of scientific lore, as in 'The Metamorphosis of Plants' and 'The Metamorphosis of Animals.' Yet he is seldom abstruse; the sententious verse he produced in such quantity is full of practical maxims:

Eigenheiten, die werden schon haften;
Kultiviere deine Eigenschaften!

or ironic comments on the ways of humanity:

Mit seltsamen Gebärden
Gibt man sich viele Pein,
Kein Mensch will etwas werden,
Ein jeder will schon was sein.

The prose counterparts of these verse epigrams are the *Maxims and Reflections* which did so much to fix Goethe's reputation as a sage. He called them 'Späne', shavings, since so many were parings from some more important bit of literary timber. It was his habit to jot them down on scraps of wrapping paper, old theatre programmes, and the backs of envelopes, and their informality, if we compare them with the polished sentences of La Rochefoucauld, is striking. They are in part a distillation of his wisdom, in part a common-place-book—full of quotations and variations on quotations, some of them, like 'Große Leidenschaften sind Krankheiten ohne Hoffnung. Was sie heilen könnte, macht sie erst recht gefährlich', pilfered from French or English collections of pithy sayings. Although the *Maxims and Reflections* range far afield, into art and science, philosophy and religion, they are for the greater part home-truths, drawn from familiar experience. 'Wer keine Liebe fühlt, muß schmeicheln lernen,' 'Es ist nichts schrecklicher als eine tätige Unwissenheit'—in sayings like these we hear Goethe clarifying his experience of himself and others, giving pointed form to truths of which we are already, but only dimly aware; they are commonplaces, touched by art.

Of Goethe's four novels, *Die Wahlverwandtschaften* (*Elective Affinities*, 1809) has worn best. To understand the stir caused by *Werther*, an effort of the imagination is needed, while the tempo and form of *Wilhelm Meisters Lehrjahre* (*Wilhelm Meister's Apprenticeship* 1795–6) and *Wilhelm Meisters Wanderjahre* (*Wilhelm Meister's Years as a Journeyman*, 1821–9) are out of line with modern taste; in *Die Wahlverwandtschaften* we have by contrast a compact, close-knit story about matters unaffected by the passage of time—the institution of marriage and the operation of natural laws in human relations. A strange enterprise, Goethe called it. There is certainly nothing quite like it in English or French literature. The title is a term from eighteenth-century chemistry, denoting the property which some compounds have of splitting up and pairing off, as if by choice, with other affined substances. Goethe defended it, but hardly explained it, by saying that he was merely transferring an analogy back to the sphere, the moral sphere, from which the scientists had originally borrowed it. He shows us a kind of elective affinity at work in two pairs of characters. Eduard and Charlotte live in more or less peaceful seclusion, filling their days with improvements to their estate, until they are joined by Eduard's friend, the Captain, and Charlotte's foster-daughter, Ottilie, brought back from boarding school because of her slow development. Charlotte and the Captain, Eduard and Ottilie fall in love and are caught up in a conflict which only Charlotte and the Captain survive. *Die Wahlverwandtschaften* is a singular blend of the lucid and the mysterious. There would be less dispute about its meaning if it merely recounted a clash between natural impulse and moral scruple, and did not also challenge our use of such handy formulae. The main characters, joined by occasional outsiders like the professional busybody

Mittler, whose mission it is to solve moral muddles, perform their evolutions under the eye of a detached but sympathetic observer. Goethe hides behind him and covers the bitter personal experiences which went into the novel with a veil of irony. Ottilie, transfigured by suffering and renunciation, achieves before her death a saintliness which Eduard cannot hope to match. He has as little talent for dying as he had for living and his last words are a rueful admission that there can be genius in everything, even in martyrdom.

Wilhelm Meister has little in common with *Die Wahlverwandt-schaften* save the symbolic quality of the action and characters. It is a vast allegory in two loosely connected parts which took Goethe over fifty years to write. It began as a realistic account of theatrical life in eighteenth-century Germany, entitled *Wilhelm Meisters Thea-tralische Sendung* (*William Meister's Theatrical Mission*, 1777), but Goethe dropped this project and when he took it up many years later approached it with a new set of ethical and literary values. The fragmentary *Theatralische Sendung* was incorporated in *Wilhelm Meisters Lehrjahre*, a 'Bildungsroman', written in stately prose, in which the theatre is no more than a confused but necessary stage in Wilhelm's progress to maturity. As an apprentice in the craft of living, he learns that self-limitation is a condition of self-fulfilment and that freedom is to be found only within the bounds of a community; he forsakes, in Schiller's view of the novel, a vague and empty ideal for a circumscribed, practical life, without thereby forfeiting his power of idealization. His subsequent development is recorded in the *Wanderjahre,* which Goethe finished in 1829 at the age of eighty. It is a compendium of his views on personal and social ethics, in the form of a miscellany of episodes, aphorisms, and extracts from diaries and letters linked by a thread of narrative. In the *Lehrjahre*, the benevolent forces operating in Wilhelm's life were symbolized by the Society of the Tower; it reappears in the *Wanderjahre*, renamed 'the Renunciants', since its members follow a code of service and self-denial and under its guidance Wilhelm moves out into wider spheres of activity. He travels with his son to the Educational Province, where the children are brought up on prin-ciples resembling Pestalozzi's 'Education through work for work'. He enters the political sphere through the agency of Baron Lenardo, who has founded a settlement of artisans, in training for the establishment of Utopian commonwealths in America and Germany, and towards the end of the novel is on the eve of departure for the New World, to start life afresh unhampered by the traditions of Europe.

Wilhelm Meister cannot be reduced to a formula—Goethe himself was not sure that he had the key to it—but it was, among other things, his way of coming to terms with the changes brought about by the French Revolution and the Industrial Revolution. In the *Lehrjahre* he formulated the type of personality best fitted to resist the stresses and strains of the new age (only to be accused of 'artistic atheism' by the Romantic writer Novalis). In the *Wanderjahre* he formulated the kind of ethics, education, and society appropriate to the changed circumstances. Both novels are the work of a sanguine, yet sceptical mind, heir to the optimism of the Enlightenment but by no means sure that humanity can be put to rights by right thinking. Wilhelm Meister, who comes to a happy end despite his aberrations and stupidities, is not Everyman; he is a special kind of being, an educable, and moreover, a lucky man. For an explanation of his nature we are directed to the Book of Samuel, where it is recorded that Saul, the son of Kish, went in search of his father's she-asses—and found a kingdom.

Although Goethe had a lifelong interest in the theatre and wrote a quantity of plays and playlets, ranging from lightweight pastorals, libretti, and satires to the massive 'Tragödie' *Faust*, he was not a dramatist, and still less a playwright, in the ordinary sense of these words. He was a poet who used drama as a way of getting to grips with experience. His best plays—*Egmont*, *Iphigenie auf Tauris*, *Torquato Tasso*, and *Faust*—are reflective and for the most part subdued in tone. Although there are vivid and powerful scenes in *Egmont* and *Faust*, passionate conflicts and *coups de théâtre* were not to Goethe's taste; his plots are such that one cannot summarize them without imposing upon them some arbitrary interpretation and his dialogue is disguised soliloquy. He completed or began these plays in his twenties and thirties when his growth was most rapid. He searched in history or legend for symbols appropriate to the problems which vexed him and projected himself into pairs of characters like

Egmont and the Prince of Orange, Iphigenie and Pylades, Tasso and Antonio, Faust and Mephistopheles; he conducted experiments with them, exposing his heroes and heroines to experience and testing out possible responses to life, or modes of accommodating personal desires, ambitions, and principles to the realities outside the self. If the plays were no more than a direct reflection of Goethe's private troubles, they would be poor entertainment. They are memorable works of art because he was able through his techniques and command of language to transmute his peculiarities into general truths of human nature which we can all understand. *Torquato Tasso* (1790) is typical of his dramatic method. It is at first sight a forbidding play. It is about the tribulations, at the Court of Ferrara, of a sixteenth-century Italian poet unfamiliar to most of us. Little happens, except for a couple of indiscretions on the part of Tasso: in the second act he quarrels with Secretary of State Antonio Montecatino and draws his sword within the precincts of the Ducal palace; in the fifth, he makes advances to the Duke's sister Lenore. The medium is blank verse and the form is of classical severity: there are five acts, all except one with five scenes, and five characters who engage, like the members of a quintet, in a series of interconnected solos and duets, varied by a few trios, a quartet, and an ensemble. The last scene, in which Tasso embraces his antagonist Antonio, is of irritating vagueness and has perplexed generations of critics. Is the play meant to be a tragedy or not? Is it about 'le malheur d'être poète' and if it is, what is the nature of his suffering? Will he, like the real Tasso, end in madness? Is he a symbol of Genius in conflict with Society, or is he a special kind of creative artist, the romantic poet? Goethe for his part made light of the play's meaning, whereas he made heavy weather of its form. No sooner had he begun it than he wondered why he had ever taken on such a task. When he put the finishing touches to it, after ten years of intermittent hard labour, his comment was: Never again! The intimate nature of the material was a major cause of trouble. *Tasso* is the most private of Goethe's plays—it was, he said, 'bone of my bone and flesh of my flesh'—and in no other do we so clearly hear him communing with himself. He had first to condense the rarefied stuff of the play so that it became visible to others and this he did by turning the original prose draft, which he found 'nebulous and sloppy', into verse—his proven cure for long-windedness and imprecision. He then had to put a safe distance between himself and his embarrassingly topical subject (his own experiences at the court of Weimar lay behind it). His method was to move away from the local and particular to the general and universal, so that the play is full of such 'maxims and reflections' as

> Es bildet ein Talent sich in der Stille,
> Sich ein Charakter in dem Strom der Welt

or

> Willst du genau erfahren was sich ziemt,
> So frage nur bei edlen Frauen an.
> Nach Freiheit strebt der Mann, das Weib nach Sitte.

Another problem was the specialized nature of his hero; Goethe had to make Tasso plausible as a poet, yet accessible to those with at most a lukewarm interest in the oddities of creative artists. He solved it by applying a veneer of irony to the serious substance of the play. His Tasso is both a maladjusted genius and an incorrigible child, the restive subject of an educational experiment made by well-meaning but far from disinterested tutors, who would if they could civilize him out of existence. 'The martyrdom of genius' was, in Schopenhauer's view, the theme of *Torquato Tasso*; it also shows us what it is like to be young and in trouble—an experience not restricted to sixteenth-century Italian poets.

Torquato Tasso, all symmetry and concentration, calls to mind a Palladian villa, whereas *Faust* is more like a cathedral—vast and rambling in structure, built over a long stretch of time in a medley of styles, in part dimly and in part brilliantly lit, symbolic as a whole of the faith which inspired it yet full of motifs which have nothing to do with faith and spring from the exuberant invention of the craftsman. Summarily described, *Faust* (1808–32) is a dramatic poem in two parts, classified as a 'tragedy', so long and complex that the theatre of Goethe's time could not cope with it. The first part, finished in 1808, was first performed in Weimar in 1829, on the occasion of Goethe's eightieth birthday and it was not until the 1890s that productions of both parts in abridged form became feasible. With the resources now available, *Faust* is more manageable as a play. Its structure—it consists of some fifty scenes linked by an argument stated in the prologue, elaborated in the body of the work, and taken up again in the finale—prefigures that of a film scenario written with an eye to the mobility of the cine-camera and the support of music. *Faust* is so often spoken of in superlatives that new-comers to it may anticipate a work of unfathomable profundity and even if they enjoy Part I may jib at Part II, which at first sight pro-mises a gruelling cultural experience. Goethe's advice to us was not to root about in the play for some underlying idea—he has after all considerately provided a crib in the shape of the Prologue in Heaven—but to abandon ourselves to the impressions, entertaining, moving, or uplifting as the case may be, which the parts make upon us. The scenes are remarkable for their vigour and variety of mood, particu-larly in Part I, which pivots around Faust's wager with Mephist-opheles, his seduction of Gretchen and murder of her brother Valentin, and Gretchen's execution for infanticide. There are re-condite passages in Part II, set at the Emperor's court and Faust's castle, with excursions to ancient Greece and a flashback to Faust's old professorial study, but it too has many lively and pointed episodes. It ranges over wide tracts of experience and embodies, in the classical Walpurgis Night and the treatment of Faust's union with Helen of Troy, some of Goethe's intimate intellectual concerns. He was well aware that he was making heavy demands on the reader and did his best, as he put it, to give the skeleton of ideas a covering of sinew, flesh, and epidermis. The result is that even the more abstract sections have a full-blooded quality and, with the possible exception of the final Chorus Mysticus, stand up well to good prose translation.

While Faust is given the most memorable lines in the play, its liveliness is due largely to Mephistopheles, possibly the best character and certainly the best acting part ever created by Goethe. In the divine scheme of things, Mephistopheles is the spirit of perpetual negation; he operates on earth as a sardonic, witty, and a sharp-tongued Devil, an arch-deflator of windy idealism. When, wearing Faust's gown and sitting in his professorial chair, he counsels the freshman—

Grau, teurer Freund, ist alle Theorie,
Und grün des Lebens goldner Baum

he is even a wise and humane Devil. When he is absent the pace of entertainment slackens; when he is present, it sharpens, and the cosmic drama is brought down to earth. Towards the end of his life, Goethe spoke of *Faust* as a kind of serious-minded jesting. Had he followed his inclination, he would have let us draw our own conclusions about the work, but he was under pressure to underpin it with philosophical props and supply some kind of guide to it. Schiller, without whose prodding and nagging the first part would never have been finished, wrote to him: 'Twist and turn as you may, the nature of the subject will force you to treat it philosophically and your imagination will have to submit to the service of a rational idea.' Goethe was only too conscious of what was expected of him. 'As the philosophers are curious about the work,' he told Schiller, 'I realize that I have to be on my best behaviour.' He ended by enclosing the story of Faust's earthly existence, which has tragic implications, within a mystery play which upends the notion of good and evil underlying the old *History of Dr. Faustus* and is the reverse of tragic. A happy ending is not only foreshadowed but virtually guaranteed by the Prologue in Heaven, in which the Lord challenges Mephistopheles, with whom he is on affectionate terms, to lead His servant Faust away from his divine source. A safe bet if ever there was one: in His creation a good man, however confused he may be, is well able to tell the right way from the wrong and any man—as the angelic chorus tells us on divine authority in the finale—is capable of redemption if he spends his life in restless endeavour. In the parallel wager with Faust which replaces the pact with the Devil in the chap-book the dice are heavily loaded against Mephistopheles. Faust's soul will be his if he can bring him to a standstill and satisfy aspirations and appetites that are by their very nature insatiable. Goethe summed them up in Faust's lines:

Werd' ich zum Augenblicke sagen:
Verweile doch! du bist so schön!
Dann magst du mich in Fesseln schlagen,
Dann will ich gern zugrunde gehn!

and thereby got himself into a difficulty from which he extricated himself by a verbal conjuring trick. At the end of the play, Faust, by now a hundred years old, blind, and on the brink of death, is busy with a vast scheme of land reclamation, while Mephistopheles is busy with a grimmer task—the digging of Faust's grave. At this point, Faust makes the last and most pardonable of his errors. He mistakes the clatter of the gravediggers' spades for the sound of his own labourers at work, and has a vision of the sturdy community that will occupy, one day, the land wrested from the sea. In anticipation of this golden moment, he has an intimation, a presentiment of happiness and satisfaction:

> Zum Augenblicke dürft' ich sagen:
> Verweile doch, du bist so schön! ...
> Im Vorgefühl von solchem hohen Glück
> Genieß' ich jetzt den höchsten Augenblick.

He dies, and after a skirmish for his soul is transported to heaven by the angelic host, leaving Mephistopheles to revile the gang of crafty smugglers who have cheated him of his due.

A poem, it has been said, is never finished, only abandoned—and so it is with *Faust*. Goethe's description of it as 'incommensurable' has not stopped numberless critics from applying to it yardsticks of one kind or another. Some are lost in admiration, others, grasping at the intellectual shadow and losing the poetic substance, reach unflattering conclusions: the play's philosophy is hollow, based on a crass belief in the self-sufficiency of man, its subject unsuited to a writer with so little religious sense, its hero a megalomaniac from first to last. Interpretations of *Faust*, however ingenious, centre upon certain simple questions. What kind of man, for example, is Faust meant to be? Is he in some way estimable or is he still the 'abshew-liches Exempel', the awful example, of the old chap-book? One thing is certain: he is a lucky man, the kind who gets away with murder. He brings to mind Goethe's couplet:

> 'Wohl kamst du durch; so ging es allenfalls.'
> Machs einer nach und breche nicht den Hals.

(6)

In so far as a dramatic tradition exists in Germany, its fount is not the inimitable Goethe but Schiller. Many a seeming innovation in the modern theatre turns out to have its roots in his theory or practice, and his bold, at times crude, stagecraft has ensured him lasting popularity. He was much given to stirring effects of an operatic nature and was a notable contriver of dramatic confrontations, like the collision between Elizabeth and Mary Queen of Scots in the third act of *Maria Stuart*. He is fertile in resounding lines and has contributed lavishly to the national stock of quotations. He is a specialist in moving or blood-curdling curtains. In his 'romantic tragedy', *Die Jungfrau von Orleans* (*The Maid of Orleans*), his Joan of Arc dies sublimely on the battlefield, flag in hand, beneath a sky suffused with a roseate glow, re-enacting the assumption of the Blessed Virgin:

> Wie wird mir—Leichte Wolken heben mich—
> Der schwere Panzer wird zum Flügelkleide.
> Hinauf—hinauf—Die Erde flieht zurück—
> Kurz ist der Schmerz, und ewig ist die Freude.

At the end of *Don Carlos*, Carlos takes leave of his stepmother and former fiancée Elizabeth of Valois, while King Philip and the Grand Inquisitor, blind and old beyond the reach of mercy, steal upon them unawares. Philip, 'kalt und still', commits them to their fate with the words:

> Cardinal, ich habe
> Das Meinige getan. Tun Sie das Ihre.

Despite his baffling plots, his long-winded characters and the densely packed blank verse he used in his later plays, Schiller was an effective dramatist from the start. His first play, *Die Räuber* (*The Robbers*), caused a riot when it was first performed in Mannheim in 1782. The theatre, according to an eye-witness, resembled a madhouse; eyes rolled, fists were clenched, and hoarse cries rang out in the auditorium; total strangers fell into each other's arms and women tottered fainting to the exit. Even to read it was a shattering experience; it convulsed the heart of Walter Scott, and William Hazlitt (it was the first play he ever read) professed himself stunned by it. *Kabale und Liebe* (*Intrigue and Love*), his third play, originally entitled *Luise Millerin*, might be thought an old-fashioned tragedy of common life and frustrated love. Nevertheless, according to Thomas Mann, when performed in Munich shortly after the First World War it whipped up an audience of reactionary bourgeois into a species of revolutionary fury. *Die Jungfrau von Orleans* is still capable of moving spectators to lengthy paroxysms of applause.

Schiller's robustness may seem surprising in a writer usually described as reflective, moved by ideas rather than experience, an idealist contemptuous of 'the empirical world' or 'the garbage of reality'. In fact, there is a vigorous strain of realism in Schiller's personality, and in his thinking about life and literature.

My limited experience [he wrote to Goethe] has taught me that you cannot make the generality of people feel good through poetry, whereas you can make them feel bad and so, it seems to me, if you can't achieve the one you must have a go at the other. You must make them uneasy, shame them out of their complacency, disquiet and dumbfound them ... Only thus will they learn to believe in the existence of poetry and to respect poets.

A variant of this principle is discernible in the theory of tragedy he formulated, in Kantian terms, in four of his essays—*On the Reason for our Pleasure in Tragic Subjects*, *On Tragic Art*, *On the Pathetic*, and *On the Sublime*. Intricate though the argument may be, it is based on a simple principle: the primary aim of tragedy is to move us. If it fails to 'convulse the heart', as it will do if the form is imperfect, it cannot begin to have those beneficial effects which Schiller attributes to it. For all his insistence that preaching and propaganda are no part of the dramatist's business (his job is to produce an aesthetically satisfying illusion), Schiller sees tragedy as a kind of therapy, a psychological experiment directed at our 'Gemüt', the totality of the inner man. He judges it by the state of mind in which it leaves the spectator. Ideally, this should be a sense of liberation, of exhilaration, induced artificially by the dramatist, who first robs us of our spiritual freedom by making an onslaught on our emotions and finally restores it by aesthetic means. With the exception of *Wilhelm Tell*, Schiller's plays are all tragedies. He had by his own confession not the slightest talent for comedy—'I am much too serious-minded,' he said—but he had the highest regard for it as an art. He goes so far as to say, in his essay *On Naïve and Sentimental Poetry*, that if comedy attained its object completely it would make tragedy superfluous, indeed impossible; it induces the free play of the mind in a less roundabout way and moves towards an even more important goal:

Its aim is no less than the highest to which man can aspire—to be free from passion, to survey himself and the world around him with constant clarity, constant tranquillity, to find everywhere more evidence of caprice than of fate and to laugh at absurdity rather than revile and bewail evil.

Schiller's intensive study of the form and function of tragedy was typical of him. In his early letters to Goethe, he made acute comparisons between his own speculative mentality and Goethe's intuitiveness. If he made an impression of *gaucherie*, especially in his earlier years, this was due to the tussle going on inside him between the philosopher and the poet; when he ought to have been philosophizing the poet crept up on him and when he wanted to write poetry the philosophical side of him took over. Goethe for his part found in Schiller's nature a strange mixture of intuition and abstraction, and thought that, on balance, the poet in him was worsted by the philosopher. 'It grieves me to think,' he told Eckermann, 'that a man with such extraordinary gifts should have tormented himself with philosophical speculations of one kind or another which could not possibly do him any good.' Admirers of Schiller take a different view and would not have him other than he was. He could not always harmonize the two sides of his nature, but when he did—in, for example, his *Wallenstein* trilogy and his treatise *Über die ästhetische Erziehung des Menschen* (*On the Aesthetic Education of Man*)—the quality of his writing, whether prose or verse, is outstanding.

Schiller was a man to whom nothing came easily, who drove himself beyond the limits of his strength as if conscious that he had little time to spare. He died of tuberculosis at the age of forty-five. He brought to literature an odd set of qualifications—in medicine and history. He studied medicine at the Duke of Württemberg's military academy, the 'Hohe Karlsschule' and was for a time an army surgeon, attached to a grenadier regiment in Stuttgart. Forbidden, after the publication of *Die Räuber*, to write any more plays, he deserted, took refuge in Mannheim, and for the next seven years existed on the charity of friends and on what he could earn from journalism and a temporary post as 'Theaterdichter' at the Mannheim National Theatre. He then forsook drama for history, chose the period he had studied when writing *Don Carlos* and began a *History of the Secession of the United Netherlands from the Spanish Government*. He never finished it, but the first volume served as a passport to a brief academic career as Professor of History at Jena. Ill health forced him to resign and thereafter, up to his death in 1805, he busied himself with drama and criticism, with the unending self-education to which he subjected himself and with the campaign of 'Kulturpolitik' in which he collaborated with Goethe. During the last phase of his life his industry was prodigious; he founded and edited two periodicals, the *Musenalmanach* and *Die Horen* (the Horae were the custodians of the gates of Olympus, personifications of order in Greek mythology); he wrote much poetry, balladesque, reflective, and satirical, six substantial essays, and a history of the Thirty Years War; he adapted and translated plays for the Weimar theatre, including works by Euripides, Shakespeare, and Racine, completed five plays, and left several dramatic projects unfinished.

Schiller's first four plays, written in his twenties, were experiments, conducted by the light of instinct, in various types of tragedy and subject matter. *Die Räuber* (1781) was planned as a domestic drama on the theme of the prodigal son, set in contemporary Germany, centred upon a younger brother, Karl Moor, who takes to banditry after his elder brother Franz has induced his father to disown him. By the time it reached the stage it had the title of tragedy, had been transposed for reasons of discretion to the sixteenth century and had been pruned of its more offensive scenes, including the bandits' attack on a nunnery and the mass rape of the nuns. It was still violent in substance and language, but the outcome was tame enough: Karl Moor gives himself up and exhorts his fellow robbers to employ their talents in a worthy cause. 'Serve a King,' he bids them, 'who fights for the rights of humanity.' *Die Räuber* was followed by the 'republican tragedy' *Die Verschwörung des Fiesko zu Genua* (*The Conspiracy of Fiesco at Genoa*, 1783), the 'bürgerliches Trauerspiel' *Kabale und Liebe* (1784), and *Don Carlos*, (1787), which Schiller called 'a dramatic poem'. Set like *Die Räuber* and *Fiesko* in the sixteenth century, *Don Carlos* is a multiple tragedy of inordinate length and complexity, with a plethora of tragic situations involving Carlos, his father, Philip of Spain, and his friend, the high-minded but over-ambitious Marquis von Posa. After a gap of ten years, during which Schiller was busy with philosophy, history, and criticism, the process of experimentation began afresh on a higher plane, conducted this time by the light of theory rather than instinct. Schiller finished the last part of *Wallenstein* in 1799 and followed it, broadly speaking at yearly intervals, with three other tragedies, *Maria Stuart*, *Die Jungfrau von Orleans*, and *Die Braut von Messina oder die feindlichen Brüder* (*The Bride of Messina or The Hostile Brothers*), and the dramatic epic *Wilhelm Tell*. These later plays display Schiller's restless ingenuity in combining the various dramatic styles, Greek, Shakespearian, and French, which he had studied and in solving technical problems of his own choosing. No sooner had he tried his hand at a 'romantic' tragedy and written *Die Jungfrau von Orleans* than he set himself an exercise in strict classical form and wrote *Die Braut von Messina*. Reverting to the theme he had already used in *Die Räuber*—the rivalry of two brothers for the same woman, in this case by a trick of fate their sister—he attempts to make the Greek notion of necessity and the Greek device of the chorus palatable to an eighteenth-century audience. Whereas in *Die Jungfrau von Orleans* he attacks our feelings directly, in *Die Braut von Messina* he puts a barrier between us and the characters; he uses the chorus as an 'ideal spectator' reminding us how to behave in the theatre and teaching us to distinguish between a work of art and a slice of life.

Despite his experimentation with dramatic form, Schiller stayed faithful to history as a source of subjects. The play of abstract historical forces does not interest him; he is concerned with the human realities which lie behind them, with the pursuit and for-feiture, the use and abuse of power which are at the heart of politics. He sees history as a moral battlefield where personalities clash and are exposed to the kind of crises and dilemmas on which drama thrives. He bends history to suit his purpose, nowhere more violently than in *Maria Stuart*. Of all his plays *Maria Stuart* (1800) is closest to Schiller's notion of ideal tragedy—concentrated and coherent in form, all the elements geared to a final and exhilarating display of moral freedom. He rejuvenates Mary and Elizabeth by a score of years, the better to motivate the personal conflict which governs the structure of the play; his Mary is a young, passionate, and sexually attractive woman, guilty of the murder of Darnley, but innocent of the crime for which she is condemned to death, the attempted assassination of Elizabeth. When the play begins, she is a prisoner in Fotheringay Castle, a prisoner too of her own illusions. One by one the avenues of escape are closed and with the signature of her death warrant by Elizabeth she experiences one of those moments of truth with which Schiller liked to confront his heroes and heroines. 'Depend upon it, Sir,' said Dr. Johnson, 'when a man knows he is to be hanged in a fortnight, it concentrates his mind wonderfully.' So it is with Mary Stuart. She shakes off her earthly ties, takes the sacrament, is given absolution, and as she goes to the scaffold sets her weeping entourage an example of sublime composure. There is an ironic epilogue; Elizabeth is left alone on the stage, deserted by the advisers on whom she has tried to unload her guilt. As the curtain falls she summons her favourite Leicester, only to be told: 'The Earl sends his excuses. He has set sail for France.'

The background of *Wallenstein* (1796–9) is the Thirty Years War. Its hero is a Bohemian soldier of fortune, commander-in-chief of the Imperial forces, a far-sighted statesman to his friends and a self-seeking traitor to his enemies, who was murdered by his own officers towards the end of the war. The dimensions of *Wallenstein* are as vast as those of *Maria Stuart* are narrow. It is a dramatic poem in three parts: a prelude, *Wallenstein's Camp*, a five-act expository play which gets its title, *The Piccolomini*, from Wallenstein's Italian adversary, Lieutenant-General Octavio Piccolomini and his son Max, and a final tragedy, *Wallenstein's Death*. It was the first of Schiller's mature plays; he began work on it nine years after finishing *Don Carlos*, determined to have done with what seemed to him the botched workmanship, crude psychology, and vague idealism of his earlier efforts. He had chosen for hero a powerful and ambitious man who could only be made plausible if the sources of his power, the high stakes for which he was playing, and the magnitude of the obstacles in his way were fully displayed. Schiller, never one for half measures, solved the problem by putting not only Wallenstein but his army and, one sometimes feels, the whole of the Thirty Years War on the stage. The framework of the trilogy may be ponderous, the canvas overloaded with detail, but the figure at its centre is the best of Schiller's dramatic portraits. He gives the illusion of depth and solidity to a character by nature shadowy, elusive, and inconstant. Wallenstein combines political realism with a well-developed capacity for self-deception; he is ruthless in his treatment of others yet greedy for their esteem, self-willed yet prone to paralysis of the will, a personality at once magnetic and repellent. For long he tries to keep his options open but is manoeuvred into a dilemma from which there is no escape. Faced with the alternatives of rebellion against the Emperor or relegation to total obscurity, he chooses rebellion, and having made his decision faces the wreckage of his plans with a composure that falls considerably short of moral grandeur. His last speech shows him still a prisoner of his illusions:

> Zu ernsthaft
> Hats angefangen, um in nichts zu enden.
> Hab es denn seinen Lauf!

Things take their course, and his meaningless conflict ends in his ignoble death. Schiller ended his prologue to *Wallenstein* with the line: 'Ernst ist das Leben, heiter ist die Kunst' ('Life is earnest, art serene') but the realities of his subject got the better of his principles; the boundaries between art and life are blurred and we are left with an overpowering sense of desolation and waste.

In his young days Schiller wrote an 'Ode to Joy' which has become, thanks to Beethoven and the Choral Symphony, his best-known poem. Although he dismissed 'An die Freude' in later life as 'a bad poem', it is in some ways a characteristic piece of Schillerian verse.

Joy is no more than the starting-point of its erratic course; it begins as a hymn, turns into a drinking song and ends as a recital of Schiller's moral ideals, in a series of resounding slogans:

> Festen Mut in schweren Leiden,
> > Hilfe, wo die Unschuld weint,
> Ewigkeit geschwornen Eiden,
> > Wahrheit gegen Freund und Feind,
> Männerstolz vor Königsthronen—
> > Brüder, gält' es Gut und Blut:
> Dem Verdienste seine Kronen,
> > Untergang der Lügenbrut!

More rarefied ideals form the stuff of his later poetry. Whereas in 'An die Freude' he had hymned Joy as the mainspring of Nature and a fount of moral energy, in 'Die Künstler' (The Artists) he extols Art as the driving force behind man's progress from savagery to civilization. The idea is elaborated in *The Aesthetic Education of Man* (1795), a treatise based on a view of art as aesthetic play, morally disinterested yet able to exert a powerful, if indirect, influence on the moral sphere. Written in the shadow of the French Revolution, it was Schiller's political testament, a counter to the ideological frenzy —that 'most terrible of Terrors'—of the revolutionary zealots. He operates with a model of humanity in which there is no cleavage between the inner and outer man and argues his way towards the concept of 'the aesthetic State' which guarantees true liberty, equality, and fraternity since it mirrors the harmonious personalities of its citizens and reconciles public and private morality. The 'aesthetic State' is less than a reality, more than a Utopia. To the question, where can such a State be found?', Schiller answers: it exists as a need in every finely tempered mind; in practice, it exists only among a few chosen spirits, expert in the art of asserting their own freedom without impairing the liberties of others.

Writing of an earlier age, the age of Milton, Samuel Johnson noted that 'there prevailed in his time an opinion that the world was in its decay, and that we have had the misfortune to be produced in the decrepitude of Nature'. The opinion lingered on into the Enlightenment, for all its show of optimism, and took the form, in Germany, of a positive obsession with ancient Greece. Greece became a symbol of those virtues in which the present was woefully deficient. Deformities of the spirit, fractured personalities, a sick society, and pervasive ugliness—these were the price paid for progress; homesick for Nature, modern man could at least console and fortify himself with ideals of simplicity, wholeness, and beauty drawn from Greek civilization. In his poem 'Die Götter Griechenlands' (The Gods of Greece), Schiller laments the passing of the Greek pantheon, the creation of an age in which nothing but beauty was sacred, when men were the more divine because their divinities were humane. The Greek gods have withered away under the cold blast of Christian monotheism; we are left with their pale reflection in art, and the hope of a Second Coming:

> Schöne Welt, wo bist du? Kehre wieder,
> Holdes Blütenalter der Natur !

(7)

For Schiller, the cult of Greece was an affair of the head; for his fellow Swabian and disciple Friedrich Hölderlin it was an affair of the heart, a mode of worship. Hellenism and Christianity, Dionysos and Jesus, ran together in his mind to produce the personal mythology in which he clothes his beliefs, thoughts, and feelings. When he was a young man, he was befriended by Schiller, who gave him practical help—he found him a post as tutor in Weimar—and well-meant counsel. Aim at simplicity and clarity, he urged him; avoid philosophical subjects and keep in touch with the world of the senses, otherwise your enthusiasm will swamp your sobriety. He might as well have recommended swimming lessons to a drowning man. Sobriety was for Hölderlin an ideal to be pursued rather than a virtue to be practised; he could find no middle ground between exaltation and depression and was in as much danger from the one as from the other. 'You can come to grief,' he said, 'as easily on the heights as in the depths.' The struggle to reconcile the richness of his dreams with the poverty of his life cost him his sanity. What began as a congenital sense of loneliness developed into total alienation; he had the first of a series of mental collapses in his early thirties and lived on for nearly forty years, an inoffensive and incurable lunatic.

Enthusiasm in search of an outlet: such was Hölderlin's nature. He fed his craving for ideals on a varied diet—on pietism, pantheism, the French Revolution, and above all Greece. His poetry is encrusted with Greek myths, gods, festivals, and place-names; when he is not writing in free rhythms, he uses Greek metres and strophes; his unfinished tragedy *Der Tod des Empedokles* (*The Death of Empedocles*) has for hero the Greek statesman, philosopher, and poet who according to legend wished to be thought a god and, so as to conceal the manner of his death, threw himself into the crater of Mount Etna; his novel *Hyperion* (1797–9) is set in modern Greece, with the revolt against the Turks in the 1770s as its background. Hölderlin was a man for whom the past was by definition happier than the present and his love of Greece was matched by his hatred of the age in which he lived; the elegies, epistles, and hymns, such as 'Brot und Wein' (Bread and Wine) and 'Der Archipelagus' (The Archipelago), which he wrote at the turn of the century are studded with images of its aridity. It is soulless, godless, and joyless; men toil like savages in their dismal factories, violating Nature instead of worshipping her, each chained to his own labour, each attentive amid the din only to his own voice, wasting their lives in restless and meaningless activity; it is time in which much happens, and little takes effect. Nowhere was 'die Unheilbarkeit des Jahrhunderts', the pernicious sickness of the age, more apparent than in Hölderlin's native land. When Hyperion revisits Germany, he compares it to a battlefield, strewn with dismembered bodies, their life-blood seeping away into the sand; wherever he looks, he finds fragments of humanity—workers, intellectuals, priests, masters, and servants—but no trace anywhere of a whole man. For Hyperion, Greece was a refuge from the ugliness of Germany; for Hölderlin it was something more—a fortifying ideal, nourishing the hope of a German renascence and of better times to come. He saw the present as an interval between a glorious past and a future in which regenerate humanity would be reunited in a true community, a time of waiting, in which the poet had a lofty and perilous mission to perform. He saw the poet as a prophet, 'a voice crying aloud in the wilderness: Prepare the way for the Lord', a mediator between God and man, a mouthpiece of nature, dedicated to 'das Höchste', the highest aspirations of mankind.

Isolation from his fellows, the temptation to make a trade of the spirit, the extremes of arrogance and self-contempt—these were the hazards he had to face. The poetic life, with its troubles and consolations, is a theme to which Hölderlin returns again and again. 'We have come too late,' he tells his friend Heinse in the epistle 'Brot und Wein'; the glories of Greece have vanished and although the old gods live on, they are far above our heads, careless if we live or die. Our life is no more than a dream of them, the present age an iron cradle in which a race of heroes, steeled by hardship and error, will surely grow to maturity. The vision quickly fades, and Hölderlin is back with his besetting doubts about the use of poets in a time of dearth:

> Indessen dünket mir öfters
> Besser zu schlafen, wie so ohne Genossen zu sein,
> So zu harren, und was zu tun indes und zu sagen,
> Weiß ich nicht, und wozu Dichter in dürftiger Zeit?

Many of his poems express intimate anxieties of this kind. In others, like the 'Schicksalslied' (Song of Destiny) which Hyperion sings to himself in a moment of dejection, Hölderlin speaks for suffering humanity, fated to plunge endlessly like a cataract into an abyss of uncertainty, and might be thought a gloomy prospect. In fact, he was little given to despair, at any rate in his poetry. Unlike some of his Romantic contemporaries, he seldom professes himself even 'half in love with easeful death' and hungers not so much for eternity as for a fuller life. His heaven is a better world, his hell a desolate place, drained of warmth and colour, cut off from the sunshine and shadow, the contrasts and contraries of the earth:

> Weh mir, wo nehm ich, wenn
> Es Winter ist, die Blumen, und wo
> Den Sonnenschein
> Und Schatten der Erde?
> Die Mauern stehn
> Sprachlos und kalt, in Winde
> Klirren die Fahnen.

Since the days of the Symbolists and Expressionists, Hölderlin's kind of imagery and his way of disrupting conventional sentence-structure have been common practice, yet he remains a difficult, and at times exasperating, poet. Some of his longer hymns and elegies are so dense with symbols that they are material for the code-breaker rather than the critic. They are a flux without clear-cut boundaries, thoughts and feelings ebbing and flowing in a semblance of logical progression. His habit of mixing plain language and cipher, of weaving together general truths and scraps of his private mythology is illustrated by the opening lines of 'Patmos':

> Nah ist
> Und schwer zu fassen der Gott.
> Wo aber gefahr ist, wächst
> Das Rettende auch.

At other times, Hölderlin writes with extreme simplicity and lucidity; he can take a threadbare subject, such as 'Homecoming', a set of commonplace metaphors and thoughts, and create out of them, through his mastery of rhythm and word-placement, a memorable poem:

> Froh kehrt der Schiffer heim an den stillen Strom,
> Von Inseln fernher, wenn er geerntet hat;
> So käm' auch ich zur Heimat, hätt' ich
> Güter so viele, wie Leid, geerntet.

> Ihr teuern Ufer, die mich erzogen einst,
> Stillt ihr der Liebe Leiden, versprecht ihr mir,
> Ihr Wälder meiner Jugend, wenn ich
> Komme, die Ruhe noch einmal wieder?

4
Romanticism

'The mysterious way leads inwards. Within us or nowhere is eternity with all its worlds, the past and the future. The outer world is the world of shadows; it casts its shadows upon the realm of light.' These words were written by a young contemporary of Goethe's, Friedrich von Hardenberg, and express that 'sense of the invisible' which was so marked a feature of German Romanticism. Hardenberg—he used the pen-name Novalis—did not take kindly to *Wilhelm Meister*. Not that he belittled it; its significance was all too clear; the Romantic element was totally submerged in it, it was artistic atheism, a *Candide* against poetry, the work of a man who handled literature as an English manufacturer handled his wares. Novalis died in 1801, in his twenties; had he lived to read the second part of *Wilhelm Meister* his judgement would have been harsher still, for the *Wanderjahre* foreshadowed a world drained of poetry and romance. The aftermath of the French Revolution, the Napoleonic Wars and the Metternich Restoration, was an unheroic age in the history of Austria and the German states, utilitarian rather than idealistic, given more to the patient accumulation and application of knowledge than to spiritual adventures. Novalis was less characteristic of it than the unromantic Friedrich Brockhaus, who began as a vendor of English wares, turned publisher, and made his encyclopedia, the *Konversationslexikon*, which first appeared in 1810, a best-seller. Against this background, the writers now known as the German Romantics appear as conservatives rather than revolutionary innovators, champions, it is true, of a new kind of poetry, but defending it by recourse to traditions deeply rooted in German literature, among them the cult of 'Innerlichkeit' and that impatience with the here and now voiced by Shelley in the lines:

> We look before and after,
> And pine for what is not.

Friedrich Nietzsche, having read a history of German Romanticism by the Danish critic, Georg Brandes, judged that the movement was consummated in the music of Schumann, Mendelssohn, Weber, Wagner, and Brahms, whereas in literature it remained a great unfulfilled promise. If we approach it by way of music and painting, where its impact is most readily experienced, or by way of the Romantic movements in England and France, we find ourselves in a strange world. On the look-out for a Victor Hugo or a Wordsworth, we end by encountering Richard Wagner, a literary figure only in so far as he was the first composer to write all his own libretti. We find ourselves among philosophers like Fichte, Schelling, and Schopenhauer, and theologians like Schleiermacher. We detect in the background pioneer psychologists like G. H. Schubert, who investigated the symbolism of dreams long before Freud, and scientists like Franz Baader or J. W. Ritter, mystics with a sufficient hold on reality to run a glass-works, like Baader, or invent the accumulator, like Ritter. In the foreground, we observe critics and translators, like August Wilhelm von Schlegel and his brother Friedrich, scholars and antiquarians like Jacob and Wilhelm Grimm, agents in the early decades of the nineteenth century of a latter-day Renaissance. Thanks to them, neglected or little-known treasures from the Germanic past, medieval epics and poetry, saga and folk-tales, folk-song and chap-books, were unearthed and edited. They brought about, moreover, a general widening of the literary horizon; new vistas—of Romance, Oriental, and English literature—were opened up with the help of translations such as the version of Shakespeare's plays begun by A. W. Schlegel and finished by Count Wolf Baudissin and Dorothea Tieck. These indirect contributions to literature overshadow the creative writing of the period. It was the work of a group of writers, born in the 1770s or early 1780s, in the main talented amateurs, who have left us a small but precious legacy of poetry, stories, and plays, and an abundance of critical disquisitions. They operated in coteries, based successively on Jena, Heidelberg, and Berlin, and were known by their opponents and imitators, before the term Romanticism was invented, as 'the modern school'.

For a manifesto of German Romanticism we have to make do with *Das Athenaeum*, a short-lived periodical (it appeared between 1798 and 1800) in which the brothers Schlegel, Ludwig Tieck, and Novalis collaborated. They were all young men, with a strong sense of their intellectual superiority, out to shock their elders rather than body forth a coherent programme. Their chosen weapon was the 'Fragment', for which the model was the French aphorist, Nicolas Chamfort, a medium well adapted to their unsystematic bent and in particular to the erratic thought processess of Friedrich Schlegel. The 'Fragment' commonly took the form of challenging assertions, such as 'Only poetry can criticize poetry' or 'We have a right to demand genius of everybody, but not expect it', intended to provoke rather than convince; it conforms to Friedrich Schlegel's definition of wit as 'an explosion of pent-up spirit' and asks to be judged not by its 'truth' but by the head of intellectual steam built up behind it. Many—such as 'Every uneducated man is the caricature of himself', 'The historian is a prophet in reverse'—are ingenious or illuminating; others, like the pseudo-definition: 'Romantic poetry is progressive, universal poetry', hint at arcane mysteries and baffled not merely the profane but the initiated, for even A. W. Schlegel could make little of the 'mystical terminology' in which his brother had wrapped the concept of Romanticism. 'He always,' complained Byron, 'seems upon the verge of meaning; and, lo, he goes down like a sunset, or melts like a rainbow.' There was nothing vague, however, about Schlegel's claim that poets should be a law unto themselves; his belief that the creative genius should be subject only to the authority of his own mind had consequences plainly to be seen in the arts of our own time. It was linked, in German Romantic doctrine, with a highly abstract and exalted notion of Art

as an agent of divine revelation and with the worship of music as
the quintessential art. Since they lived through one of the richest
periods in the history of European music, it is hardly surprising
that many writers and thinkers of the period should have been
obsessed by music. It shapes their view of literature, infiltrates their
philosophy and many of them, moreover, were involved in it practi-
cally—as composers, as agents of the Bach and Handel revival of the
1820s, and as champions of moderns like Beethoven and ancients
like Palestrina.

(2)

It was the sacred music he heard in Dresden that moved Heinrich
von Kleist to write *Die heilige Cäcilie oder Die Gewalt der Musik*
(*Saint Cecilia or the Power of Music*), the story of a miracle worked
by an orchestra of nuns. His gentle instrumentalists contrast sharply
with Hoffman's creation, the crazy and embittered Kapellmeister
Johannes Kreisler, who is more typical of the musicians in German
Romantic fiction; he ends up in a monastery, a refugee from the
life to which he cannot accommodate himself, secure at last from the
demonic power of music. Kreisler is sanity itself compared with the
totally alienated poet whose life and opinions are recorded in one
of the gloomier products of Romantic fancy, *Nachtwachen von
Bonaventura* (*Bonaventura's Night Watches*). The book appeared
anonymously in 1804 and was probably written by Friedrich Gottlob
Wetzel, an obscure medical student and disciple of the nature-
philosopher Schelling. It is either an ingenious travesty or the authentic expression of a disillusioned idealist's self-contempt and despair.
It shows us, through the distorted vision of an unsuccessful writer,
inmate of a madhouse, but permitted, since he is thought harmless,
to function as a night-watchman, a world drained of value and sense,
with nothing beyond it to redeem its emptiness. Nothing, least of all
German idealism, escapes his corrosive irony; it eats into the fabric
of life itself. The strain of melancholy we know as 'Weltschmerz',
born of frustrated hopes and fallacious ideals, running through
Romantic literature, is heard with brutal clarity: 'It is a greater
thing to hate than to love; the man who loves, desires; the man who

hates is sufficient unto himself and needs no more than the hatred in his heart.'

Kreuzgang goes his rounds in a city of dreadful night. It seems remote from the idyllic region pictured by Novalis in his *Hymnen an die Nacht* (*Hymns to Night*, 1800), a poetic sequence, partly in rhythmic prose, full of an insatiable 'hunger for eternity', yet the two zones are not, after all, so far apart. Heaven and Hell were born together, if we are to believe William Blake, and Bonaventura's nihilism was the price paid for the soaring idealism and utopian dreams that filled Novalis's mind. He shows some of the characteristic marks of European Romanticism, magnified and distorted by the circumstances of his life and the climate of ideas in which he was bred. He was the eldest of eleven children, most of them short-lived. His father, an ex-soldier with residual military tastes, was director of a Saxon salt-mine; his mother was a devout member of the Moravian Church, the 'Herrenhuter'. His education was practical: he was trained as a lawyer and also studied geology and engineering. His interest in the arts and in the craft of letters was marginal; his reading, outside philosophy, theosophy, and the natural sciences, was limited. He speaks much of 'Poesie' but in the Novalis code this means the creative imagination rather than a form of literature. The experience which underlies much of his work was the death, shortly after her fifteenth birthday, of his fiancée Sophie von Kühn, followed a few months later by the death of his favourite brother. Before long (what he felt for Sophie, he said, was not so much love as religion), he was again engaged and at the time of his death, from tuberculosis, he was on the verge of marriage and a career in the administration of the Saxon salt-mines. From the death-cult celebrated in the *Hymns to Night* and remarks such as: 'Life is a sickness of the spirit', he might be thought a morbid necromancer. To see him whole, however, is to perceive a vital specimen of what Thomas Mann called 'leidenschaftlich unbedingte Jugend' (passionately uncompromising youth), confident in the ability of ideas to change the world, expounding visionary plans for mankind with eyes fixed not on the listener but on infinity. Argue with him and he replies: 'Only an artist can guess the meaning of life' and 'Nothing is more attainable to the mind than infinity'.

He wrote, in addition to the *Hymns to Night*, a group of pietist hymns, two unfinished novels, two collections of 'fragments', *Blütenstaub (Pollen)* and *Glauben und Liebe (Faith and Love)*, and a tract entitled *Die Christenheit oder Europa*. In this, he looked back upon medieval Christendom as a golden age, lamented its disruption by the Reformation and the secular philosophies which issued from it and proclaimed a millennium in which Europe would once more be united by a common faith. He hit upon the same symbol as Blake for the forces threatening the soul of man; Blake speaks of Satanic Wheels and Mills, Novalis of the dreary creaking of a monstrous great mill, driven by the current of chance, to which philosophy has reduced the infinitely creative music of the universe. His gospel, compact of Christianity and mythology, is even less clear than Blake's, the outlines of his millennium even more blurred than those of Blake's Jerusalem. In his novel, *Heinrich von Ofterdingen* (pub. 1802), he expands his personal insights and moods, as was his way, into a message for humanity at large. It is an allegory—Novalis called it 'an apotheosis of poetry'—with an idealized medieval setting, its hero the legendary poet credited in the Romantic period with the authorship of the *Nibelungenlied*. It is dense with symbols, the best known of them the Blue Flower, which, in Germanic folk-lore, had the property of opening the eyes of its wearer to the whereabouts of buried treasure. In the novel it stands for many things, among them the goal of Heinrich's quest and the yearning which impels him on his way; the subject of many an irreverent parody, it has come to be a symbol of German Romanticism itself. The first part of *Heinrich von Ofterdingen* was entitled 'Die Erwartung' (Promise) and shows Heinrich's initiation into the mysteries of poesy. The unfinished second part, 'Die Erfüllung' (Fulfilment) was intended to move from the personal to the universal plane, projecting a vision of a new age in which 'world becomes dream, dream becomes world' and imagination reigns supreme.

Novalis's own imagination was closely linked with his restless intellect, which he applied indiscriminately to simple and complex things; even the carving and eating of meat, we learn from his notebooks, was to be the occasion for anatomical observations. The images which proliferate in his poetry and novels are so cerebral, so

remote from nature and human activity, that those unresponsive
to their message will turn instead to his fragments, especially those,
such as 'Every Englishman is an island' or 'Hope is a distant joy,
presentiment a distant idea, fear a distant grief' which make an
intellectual point. Only recently has it become clear how much
in his work that seems strange to us was familiar to him from the
practices and symbolism of the Moravian Brethren. For all his Catholic leanings, he remained something of a sectarian, the poet and the
theologian in him at loggerheads, the one searching for a *lingua
franca*, the other speaking to the elect in a private language.

(3)

'Where there are children,' said Novalis, 'you have a golden age.'
He wants us to approach literature with a child's sense of wonder
and accept, as 'the canon of poetry', the fanciful or supernatural
tale, the 'Märchen'. By one of the happier accidents of literary
history, the most celebrated by-product of German Romanticism
proved to be a collection of such stories, known to us as *Grimms'
Fairy Tales*. The first volume of the *Kinder- und Hausmärchen*
(*Nursery and Household Tales*) collected by Jacob and Wilhelm
Grimm appeared in 1812, dedicated to Frau Elisabeth von Arnim
and intended as a Christmas offering for her small son. It was an
acknowledgement of the Grimms' debt to two Romantic writers:
Frau Elisabeth's brother, Clemens Brentano, who had aroused their
interest in folk-tales, and her husband, Achim von Arnim, who had
found a publisher for them. In its original form, with its apparatus
of notes and variants, the collection was better fitted for the study
than the nursery. It was the result of sober research, tempered
by Romantic notions of childhood and folk-literature, on the part
of two archetypal German scholars who devoted their long lives
to the study of Germanic antiquity and produced, despite the inter-
ruptions and frustrations caused by the Napoleonic Wars and the
ensuing reaction, a succession of pioneer works in the fields of
literature, mythology, language, and legal history. For them, folk-
tales were the detritus of ancient myths, beliefs, and usages, to be
sifted and handled with care, and they applied to them the technique
they had learnt from the celebrated jurist Karl von Savigny who

taught them law at the University of Marburg. Determined to remain faithful to the oral tradition by which the tales had been preserved, they took only a fraction of the two hundred they collected from printed sources; most were taken down verbatim by themselves or their collaborators from story-tellers in Hesse, Westphalia, and further afield, many of them being literally old wives' tales. Wilhelm Grimm was chiefly responsible for preparing the stories for publication; he did not meddle with the substance, but tried in successive editions to match the form to the taste of young readers; enlivening stodgy narrative with direct speech and rhymes, where possible giving the tales an arresting beginning, a coherent middle, and a happy end. Sometimes the happy ending is unquestionable: Hänsel and Gretel, for example, are reunited with their parents, after which 'there was an end to all care and they lived together in pure joy'. Sometimes it takes a macabre form: in *Sneewittchen*, Snow-White's godless and cruel stepmother is forced to don red-hot iron slippers and dance until she falls down dead. Sometimes it is reached by horrific detours, as in the Low German *Von dem Machandelboom* (*The Juniper Tree*), a relic, so the Grimms thought, of Nordic and Eastern resurrection myths: a child, killed by his stepmother and served up to his father, returns as a bird singing a tell-tale song from the branches of a juniper tree, contrives the stepmother's death (she is crushed by a millstone), changes back into human shape, and lives happily ever after with his father and sister.

The suitability for children of tales such as this was, of course, contested, especially after the appearance in 1825 of a cheap, abridged, illustrated edition, for which the model was an English selection entitled *German Popular Tales*, translated by Edgar Taylor and illustrated by George Cruikshank. But the Grimms had no misgivings. The stories were, after all, echoes from an age of innocence, before Man and Nature were estranged, and fundamentally wholesome. The changes produced in them from age to age by the weathering effect of time were natural and acceptable, but arbitrary changes in deference to particular tastes, doctrines, or scruples were deplorable; they destroyed the authenticity and poetry of the stories and were moreover pointless, given the robust imagination of the normal child.

(4)

The possibilities of the 'Märchen' as a literary form had been realized long before the *Kinder- und Hausmärchen* appeared. In the fantastic tale, the Romantic writer could go his transcendental way without impediment to his imagination and use the supernatural as a cipher in which to encode messages of entertaining ambiguity. Sophisticated fairy-tales like Adelbert von Chamisso's *Peter Schlemihls wundersame Geschichte* (*The Strange History of Peter Schlemihl*) and Friedrich de la Motte Fouqué's *Undine* are parables, resembling to this extent Mary Shelley's *Frankenstein or The Modern Prometheus*, written in the same period and inspired by a collection of German ghost stories. Chamisso and Fouqué base their stories on the assumption that man's most precious, and most burdensome possession is his soul. Undine is a water sprite, daughter of a Mediterranean sea-prince, the ward and niece of a Germanic forest stream, Kühleborn, who, Proteus-like, can change his shape at will; she is in search of a soul, which she can only acquire by winning the love of a mortal. Peter Schlemihl is an all-too-human being, ready enough to sell his shadow to the Devil as a short cut to wealth and prestige, who resists the temptation to go a stage further and part with his soul. Neither the soul which Undine achieves, nor that which Schlemihl safeguards has, however a purely religious significance. What Undine obtains is a passport to mortality, to love, compassion, and suffering, rather than a guarantee of immortality. What Peter Schlemihl retains after he has lost his shadow and his money is a core of integrity which enables him to come to terms with himself and life.

Undine (1811) has an involved and libretto-like plot, which has been turned to account in opera by Hoffmann and Lortzing, in drama by Giraudoux, and in ballet by Henze. Fouqué recounts, under cover of a fairy-tale, a marital disaster, involving Undine, her knight-errant husband, Huldbrand von Ringstetten, and the other woman in the situation, Bertalda; after they have been manoeuvred into an uneasy *ménage à trois* in the knight's Black Forest castle, Undine parts from her faithless husband and plunges back into her natural element, the waters of the Danube. Huldbrand marries

Bertalda, but before the marriage can be consummated Undine returns to him; he dies in ecstasy in her arms and she is changed into a rivulet flowing round his grave. Fouqué's style may be long-winded and, as befits the story, soulful, yet his Undine is a memorable character: an elemental child-wife, unfit to bear the burden of womanhood, a misfit in human society, the innocent victim and agent of a misfortune for which nobody was really to blame. In the words of Father Heilmann, the priest who buried her husband: 'It could not have turned out any other way.'

The tone of *Peter Schlemihl* (pub. 1814) is matter-of-fact; entertaining episodes flow from Peter's shadowless predicament and the fairy-tale motifs—the bottomless purse, the cap of invisibility, and the seven-league boots—are woven neatly into the action. We suspend disbelief in his strange tale the more readily because his tormentor is a plausible and, despite the antique cut of his grey coat, a modern Devil: a malicious twister rather than a symbol of Evil, whom Peter resists from distaste as much as moral scruple. His dealings with the Devil leave him penniless and unwed, bereft of shadow but intact of soul. He finds refuge in a hermit's cell in the desert, and consolation in the exploration of Nature. In the magic boots put in his way by benevolent destiny he scours the world as a botanist and geographer: a curious mode of salvation, based on Chamisso's voyage round the world on a Russian expedition and his later occupation as Director of the Botanical Gardens in Berlin. He came of an *émigré* family, driven out of Champagne by the French Revolution, fought for Prussia during the Napoleonic Wars, and wrote *Peter Schlemihl* in 1813 during a disturbed and restless period in his life. To see the story as a political allegory, or the lost shadow merely as a symbol of Chamisso's rootlessness is, however, to oversimplify their significance. He refused to supply a key to the story, leaving us to deduce the meaning of the shadow from the effects of its loss: the false pretences and hole-in-corner existence to which Peter is reduced, the derision, suspicion, and fear he arouses in his fellows.

The figure who bedevils the life of Nathanael, the student hero of E. T. A. Hoffmann's story *Der Sandmann* (1817), resembles Peter Schlemihl's incubus inasmuch as he too wears at his first appearance a grey coat of antique cut. He is the old lawyer Coppelius, harmless enough in our kind of reality, but built up into a malign force by Nathanael's disturbed mind. *Der Sandmann* has most of the qualities which made Hoffmann a virtuoso of the fantastic tale: the crude style, tempered by touches of irony, the alternate assault on our credulity and withdrawal into rational explanations, the ability to create a world in which the bounds between the real and the imaginary are obliterated. It is one of Hoffmann's *Nachtstücke* (*Nocturnes*), the title of his second collection of stories, in which he transformed the 'Märchen' by locating the supernatural in the dark recesses of the mind, rather than in some shadowy transcendental zone. Nathanael is an artist figure, one of many in Hoffmann's tales, a mediocre writer with an uncontrolled imagination; he carries over into manhood his childish terrors, centred upon the Sandman, the bogey who, according to the family nurse, punished disobedient infants by serving up their eyes to his own children. It is a derangement of his vision that leads him to madness and suicide; he projects his fantasies upon the everyday figures around him, confusing his fiancée Klara—serene and rational to others, cold and prosaic to him—with the life-size walking and talking doll created by the optician Coppola and Professor Spollanzani, those forerunners of many a sinister foreign inventor in science fiction. Like Mary Shelley, whose *Frankenstein* appeared in the same year, 1817, as *Der Sandmann*, Hoffmann uses a motif derived from the mechanical figures in vogue in the late eighteenth century. Without his automaton Olympia the story would lose much of its point; she enables Hoffmann to indulge his irony at the expense, in particular, of egocentric writers; totally passive and barely articulate, she provides, in Nathanael's eyes, an ideal audience and unlike Klara, who was bored stiff by his stories and poems, she patiently endures, for hours at a time, his tedious recitations.

The Sandman was used by Delibes for his ballet *Coppélia* and by Offenbach's librettists, together with *The Lost Reflection* and *Councillor Krespel*, in *Les Contes d'Hoffmann*. It is chiefly through music that Hoffmann lives on today, especially in Offenbach's opera and Tchaikovsky's ballet-suite *Casse-Noisette*, based on *Nutcracker and Mouse King*. A fitting mode of survival, for Hoffmann was, among other things, a fluent if unoriginal composer. He worked for five years as a musical director in Bamberg and Dresden when his career—he was a lawyer in Prussian service—was interrupted by the Napoleonic Wars, and it was during this period of his life that he wrote his first stories. His writing, to which he turned as a means of making money, proved his surest method of keeping his balance in the treble life he contrived to lead. He had a deep interest in abnormal psychology, studied the behaviour of the mentally deranged by visiting the Sankt Getreu asylum and applied his observations in some of his best tales. In *Das Fräulein von Scuderi*, (1818), a crime story set in seventeenth-century Paris, soberly narrated by Hoffmann's standards, he uses the 'Doppelgänger' theme. The criminal Cardillac, is a split personality, by day a respected gold-smith, by night a psychopath, driven by a subconscious urge to avenge his mother's outraged virtue; it takes the form of an obsessive attachment to the objects he creates and murderous hatred of those to whom he has reluctantly sold them. When he is killed by an intended victim, his apprentice and his daughter's lover, Olivier Brusson, is wrongly accused of his murder; he is saved by the inter-vention of the seventy-three-year-old novelist, Mlle Madeleine de Scudéry, who convinces Louis XIV of his innocence. According to two early Victorian translators of *Tales from the German*, John Oxenford and C. A. Feiling, Hoffmann's aim was 'to point out the ill effects of a morbid desire after an imaginary world, and a distaste for realities'. Primed as we are nowadays with psychology, we are unlikely to see his purpose so plainly. Nevertheless, stories like *Der Sandmann* and *Das Fräulein von Scuderi* project a simple enough view of life—as a battle between Good and Evil. Hoffmann frightens us, the better to comfort us at the finish. The ending of *Der Sand-mann*, however perfunctory, is undoubtedly happy: Klara, well rid of Nathanael with his incessant inner conflicts, finds domestic bliss with a more suitable partner. Olivier, in *Das Fräulein von Scuderi*, marries Cardillac's daughter and establishes himself, with her dowry, as a prosperous goldsmith in Geneva: we are back in the world of the 'Märchen', with Mlle de Scudéry playing the part of a Good, if ancient, Fairy.

(5)

O, for an age so sheltered from annoy,
That I may never know how change the moons
Or hear the voice of busy common sense!

These lines from Keats's 'Ode on Indolence' would make a fitting
motto for *Aus dem Leben eines Taugenichts* (*From the Life of a
Good-for-Nothing*, 1826), Joseph von Eichendorff's blithe variant of
the 'Märchen'. The *Taugenichts* is everyman's idea of what
Romantic fiction ought to be: it takes us out of ourselves into an
Austro-Italian dreamland of enchanting castles, rustling forests, purl-
ing streams, and a Danube that is for ever blue. We are swept along
on breathless journeys, caught up in elopements and pursuits, be-
mused by mistaken identities and transvestism of the innocent kind.
The story, interspersed with songs, echoing to a positive orchestra of
strings, woodwind, and horns, resembles the scenario of a Viennese
'Singspiel', with an engaging clown for hero, an orphan maid for
heroine, and a cast of counts, countesses, poets, painters, students,
servants, and rustics. The style is relaxed, the humour unforced, the
tone ironical. The title is as misleading as the plot, for the ne'er-do-
well hero does, in the end, very well indeed. A miller's son, his
assets are his fiddle, his charm, and a zest for life matched only by
his distaste for work. He sets out as a wandering minstrel, has two
sinecures, as gardener and toll-keeper, bestowed upon him by a
countess who takes a fancy to him, becomes involved in her
daughter's elopement, journeys to Rome and back, and takes leave of
us on the verge of marriage and a more or less settled existence in the
diminutive estate given him by his patrons. The 'Taugenichts' looks
like an innocent abroad, but the way he tells his story bespeaks a
remarkably well-stocked mind; the mask is that of an artless miller
boy, the features behind it those of a Romantic aristocrat.

Aus dem Leben eines Taugenichts was Eichendorff's farewell to
his youth. He started it in 1816, at the age of twenty-eight, when the
shades of the prison house were beginning to close around him;
after an unexacting life as a law student and as an officer during the
dying stages of the Napoleonic Wars, he was about to enter the
Prussian civil service. In effect, he harmonized his career—he ended

it in charge of Catholic affairs in the Berlin 'Kultusministerium'—and his writing without difficulty and is the least problematic of the German Romantics. Generations of Germans have identified lyrical poetry with his kind of verse—tuneful, subdued, recording, like Guido the painter's song in the *Taugenichts*, fleeting moods:

> Schweigt der Menschen laute Lust:
> Rauscht die Erde wie in Träumen
> Wunderbar mit allen Bäumen,
> Was dem Herzen kaum bewußt,
> Alte Zeiten, linde Trauer,
> Und es schweifen leise Schauer
> Wetterleuchtend durch die Brust.

He had a store of poetic recipes, derived in part from Arnim and Brentano's collection of folk-poems *Des Knaben Wunderhorn* (*The Boy's Magic Horn*, 1805–8), to which he contributed; one of them, used for the theme-song of the *Taugenichts*, begins:

> Wem Gott will rechte Gunst erweisen,
> Den schickt er in die weite Welt,
> Dem will er seine Wunder weisen
> In Berg und Wald und Strom und Feld

and ends:

> Den lieben Gott laß ich nur walten;
> Der Bächlein, Lerchen, Wald und Feld
> Und Erd' und Himmel will erhalten,
> Hat auch mein Sach' aufs best bestellt!

'Der frohe Wandersmann' ('The Happy Wanderer') as he later entitled it is a pilgrim song, proclaiming a serene belief in the rightness of things which fills even the make-believe world of *Aus dem Leben eines Taugenichts*.

(6)

A world as make-believe as Eichendorff's confronts us in the stories and plays of Heinrich von Kleist. He created it in his own image: born without a sense of direction or balance, he found life a labyrinth to which reason, faith, and feeling were uncertain guides, a strange institution in which virtue seldom went unpunished and reasonable expectations were seldom fulfilled. There is no better introduction to Kleist than his anecdote *Über das Marionettentheater* (*On the Marionette Theatre*); written with unwonted delicacy, it is the lament of a man top-heavy with thought, envious of the puppet's unconscious grace and the poise of the performing bear he describes, effortlessly parrying the clumsy thrusts of his human opponent. Kleist had power in plenty but was short of grace. A single image, of Venus 'toute entière à sa proie attachée', suffices Racine to convey the ferocity of love; Kleist takes seventy gruelling lines to spell it out in his tragedy *Penthesilea*; his deluded Amazon queen hunts down her lover Achilles with her hounds, buries her teeth in his white breast, and emerges from the unsavoury meal with dripping jowls. Neither Penthesilea, nor the abject heroine of *Das Kätchen von Heilbronn* ('a great historical drama of chivalry'), nor the blood-thirsty Germanic chieftain Arminius in *Die Hermannsschlacht* (*The Battle of the Teutoburger Forest*) are likely to endear themselves to the world at large. At the other extreme we have the two comedies *Amphitryon* and *Der zerbrochene Krug* (*The Broken Pitcher*) and Kleist's last play *Prinz Friedrich von Homburg*; here this singularly uneven writer distances himself from his fantasies and fixed ideas, weaving them into richly textured works of art. In *The Prince of Homburg* (1810) a choice of evils leads for once to a right decision, and a happy outcome. The setting is seventeenth-century Brandenburg, the Prince a cavalry general who disobeys orders and is condemned to death. His fate is placed in his own hands: if he admits the justice of the sentence he will be executed, if he denies it he will be spared; he accepts his punishment, whereupon an all-wise Great Elector tears up the death warrant. The play resists easy interpretation, but the description of it as 'a parable of resurrection' is as apt as any; through the figure of the Prince, a man *in extremis*, swinging between rapture and despair, degradation and sublimity, delusion and truth, we see Kleist coming to terms with his most intractable problem—death.

Kleist seems to have applied three principles of war—concentration, mobility, and surprise—to the construction of his stories. Scorning manoeuvre, he employs his opening sentences and paragraphs in a frontal assault on the theme, and then develops it with economy of force and sustained momentum. A monstrous occurrence, a convulsion of nature—the earthquake which devastated Santiago in 1647—is the starting-point of *Das Erdbeben in Chili* (1807). A young couple, condemned to death for illicit love, are saved by the earthquake and enjoy an interlude of illusory happiness, but the earthquake provokes a wave of religious hysteria and the couple end by being clubbed to death by a fanatic. They are victims of that perverse fate which

> Frowns in the storm with angry brow
> But in the sunshine strikes the blow.

A convulsion of another kind is recorded in *Michael Kohlhaas* (1808). It is the story of a sixteenth-century German horse-dealer, a peaceable and model citizen, whose sense of justice, once outraged, turns him into a ruthless avenger; he is outlawed and beheaded, but not before his wrongs have been redressed. He dies content; he has made his point.

The story of Kleist's last days is an example of nature imitating art. In the summer of 1811 he sent the King of Prussia a humble petition, complaining that his newspaper, the *Berliner Abendblätter*, had been ruined by official interference and asking for compensation or a civil-service post. The King bore in mind that Kleist's family had supplied a score of generals and marshals to the Prussian army and that Kleist himself had served for seven years in the Regiment of Guards. He offered him command of a company or an appointment as one of his personal adjutants. Kleist turned the offer down; a man who pursued glory as relentlessly as his contemporary Horatio Nelson, he had by then lost hope of achieving it either in literature or war. Struck, in his earlier days, by Zoroaster's doctrine that the things most worthy of a man were to plant a tree, kill an enemy, and breed a child, he had defined his three objectives as a child, a fine poem, and a great deed. The third of these was within his grasp. He made a suicide pact with an acquaintance, Frau Henriette Vogel, who believed herself—in error—incurably ill, and resolved that his plan for dying should be more efficient than his abortive plans for living. On the shore of the Wannsee, after lunch on 20 November

1811, he shot Frau Vogel through the left breast and himself through the mouth. Neither was disfigured. His Romantic acquaintances reacted variously to his death; Arnim thought he should have heeded the good advice given him; Brentano spoke of his lovelessness and boundless conceit; Fouqué, more charitable, prayed for his soul.

Kleist is commonly regarded as a lone wolf on the fringe of the Romantic pack. To an older contemporary like Goethe, however, he embodied the most distasteful side of Romanticism—its morbidity. A generation later, Heinrich Heine had Kleist among others in mind when he said: 'Beyond doubt there is a curse on German poets.' Heine, while conceding occasional virtues to the Romantics, deplored the life-denying strain in them. Nowadays we are readier to see the Romantic generation as a whole, to see the expanse of new ground they opened up, to acknowledge how much that we take for granted in modern writing was due to their labours.

5
The Mid-Nineteenth Century

IN *Die romantische Schule* (*The Romantic School*), Heinrich Heine
looked back, half in mockery, half in affection, at the movement
whose heritage he exploited in his *Buch der Lieder* (*Book of Songs*).
This collection of his early verse, published in 1827, made him the
best known of all German poets. He has reached many of us through
the Lieder of the nineteenth-century composers; countless translators have tried their hand at him, attracted by his clear word-
pictures, his apparently artless rhythms and rhymes; George Eliot's
admiration for his nimble prose, and Matthew Arnold's for his
prowess as a warrior in humanity's war of liberation are imprinted
on the English literary memory. He was a natural outsider in the
Germany of his day. He was a Jew, turned Christian in his twenties
since all the professions save medicine would otherwise have been
barred to him. He spent nearly half his life in Paris, one of the
company of German exiles who found refuge there after the July
Revolution of 1830. Caustic on paper and in speech, he was a talented
maker of enemies. His feuds and his attachments, his running battle
with the German and Austrian censorship, his eccentric *ménage* in
the rue d'Amsterdam, his spiritual odyssey and his physical suffering
have provided his numerous biographers with rich material. His
personality emits interesting dissonances: Gérard de Nerval, who
saw much of him in his last years, found him both tender and cruel,
affirmative and sceptical, an ancient and a modern. Nearer the mark

is Schumann's description of him as 'ein ironisches Männchen', an ironical little fellow. He saw life as a tragi-comedy, mounted by a divine impresario with an unfathomable sense of humour, in which he played a variety of parts. The last and most improbable of these was as martyr-hero, facing the pain of his last years with unabated irony, his body decrepit, his mind more active than ever. He offers us a choice of last words, of which the best known, thanks to the Goncourt brothers, is probably the least authentic; asked how things stood between him and his Maker, he is reported to have said: 'Dieu me pardonnera, c'est son métier.' A final wish for pencil and paper has a truer ring. Heine was a highly professional writer, admirable for the toughness with which he overcame the obstacles in his way, some set up by his temperament, some by his time, and some by the Romantic tradition within which he began to write.

His assets were a teeming imagination, a restless brain, and a sharp awareness of reality. His problem was to mobilize them in the service of a new kind of poetry, fit to encompass the whole of life, in and around him, in all its variety. He began as a song-writer and worked his way, despite false starts and frustrating détours, towards a lyrical realism rare in nineteenth-century literature. He wrote over 300 songs, many of them variations on the theme of unrequited love, and those who know only this side of him have been puzzled by his enduring appeal. 'How,' asked his English translator Humbert Wolfe, 'has this poet who had but two strings and but one tune, fastened himself on the imagination of the world?' But Heine wrote the greater part of his poetry towards the end of his life, between 1844 and 1856, and to see it whole is to marvel at its breadth rather than its limits. In his middle period he was fertile in ballads, satires, and topical verse; in his last poems his range was no less wide and the emotional fantasies of his earlier years gave way to the direct and powerful expression of an all too real anguish.

Apart from ballads and two cycles of 'North Sea' poems, (*Die Nordsee*), the *Buch der Lieder* is a collection of lyrical miniatures. Many have become anthology pieces, like 'Auf Flügeln des Gesangs' ('On the wings of song') or popular songs, like 'Die Lorelei'; but they are best read in their original settings, the artful sequences in which Heine strung them together. That favourite target of composers:

> Du bist wie eine Blume,
> So hold und schön und rein;
> Ich schau' dich an, und Wehmut
> Schleicht mir in's Herz hinein.

loses much of its intolerable sweetness when flanked by its drier neighbours in *Die Heimkehr* (*The Homecoming*). Heine opens this cycle by comparing himself to a child in the dark, singing to keep his spirits up. Then, without explanatory title and followed by the acrid lyric 'Mein Herz, mein Herz ist traurig, doch lustig leuchtet der Mai', comes the poem beginning:

> Ich weiß nicht, was soll es bedeuten,
> Daß ich so traurig bin;
> Ein Märchen aus alten Zeiten,
> Das kommt mir nicht aus dem Sinn.

We now know it as 'Die Lorelei' and accept it as a piece of folk-lore about a Rhenish siren, but it is also one of the many songs about song in which Heine makes poetry of his own poetic troubles.

In the *Buch der Lieder* Heine was spellbound, yet exasperated, by folk-song; he had so much to say that it could not express. He makes no secret of his impatience with it: he creates a Romantic mood only to shatter it in a brutal last line or verse; he chides himself and parodies his own clichés, his moonshine, roses, and nightingales. He makes an art of folkish simplicities, inserting between two tearful lyrics the ironic lines:

> Ein Jüngling liebt ein Mädchen,
> Die hat einen Andern erwählt;
> Der Andre liebt eine Andre,
> Und hat sich mit dieser vermählt.
>
> Das Mädchen heiratet aus Ärger
> Den ersten, besten Mann,
> Der ihr in den Weg gelaufen;
> Der Jüngling ist übel daran.
>
> Es ist eine alte Geschichte,
> Doch bleibt sie immer neu;
> Und wem sie just passieret,
> Dem bricht das Herz entzwei.

The poem is from a sequence of sixty-five poems, entitled *Lyrisches Intermezzo* (*Lyrical Interlude*) because it originally appeared sandwiched between two tragedies. It was from *Lyrisches Intermezzo*, in which Heine, as he put it, portrayed Eros and Psyche in a variety of postures, that Schumann chose the sixteen poems for his *Dichterliebe* (*A Poet's Love*). The words cry out for music to give them body and Schumann gave them their perfect setting; no other composer has caught so well Heine's modulations, from sweetness to ferocity, from Romantic reveries to harsh awakenings. The last poem of *Lyrisches Intermezzo*, and of *Dichterliebe*, tells of the monstrous coffin, dumped by twelve giants in the sea, in which Heine resolved to bury 'his old and evil songs, his bad, deceitful dreams'. It took him nearly twenty years to banish them and get to poetic grips with the realities around him.

In the *Neue Gedichte* (*New Poems*, 1844) we find, alongside the recurring love lyrics and romances, bitter comments on contemporary happenings, like the revolt of the Silesian weavers in 1844, the year the collection was published. It was in the *Neue Gedichte* that the best of all German political satires first appeared—*Deutschland. Ein Wintermärchen* (*Germany. A Winter's Tale*). Within vague narrative boundaries—the poem is based on a journey made to his homeland in 1843—Heine manoeuvres freely, engaging with a withering fire a variety of targets: Prussianism, clerical obscurantism, bogus patriotism, and the unreality of German politics:

> Franzosen und Russen gehört das Land,
> Das Meer gehört den Briten,
> Wir aber besitzen im Luftreich des Traums
> Die Herrschaft unbestritten.

> Hier üben wir die Hegemonie,
> Hier sind wir unzerstückelt;
> Die andern Völker haben sich
> Auf platter Erde entwickelt.

The form of *Deutschland* is foreshadowed in *Atta Troll. Ein Sommernachtstraum* (*Atta Troll. A Midsummer Night's Dream*, 1843). This comic epic has for its hero a dancing bear, whose escape from his captors, reunion with his family, pursuit, and death give continuity to Heine's free-ranging tale. He called it a purposeless fantasia, 'the last free woodland song of Romanticism', but he spends half of it in attacking the crude tendentious poetry and demagogy of the time. A native of the Pyrenees (his den is in Roncevalles, where Roland made his last stand) Atta Troll is nevertheless a most Germanic bear; part liberal, part Philistine, misanthropic yet idealistic, right-thinking but wrong-headed, he preaches confused doctrines of liberty and equality and brings up his children in the knowledge of the Great Polar Bear, who dwells with his bearish saints in his ursine Heaven. Heine is at his most inventive in these two long poems. His easily flowing quatrains—he uses ballad metre in *Deutschland* and in *Atta Troll*, the Spanish line we know from Longfellow's *Hiawatha*—are full of surprises. He takes shameless liberties with the virtue of German poetic diction, using everyday speech and, when effect requires it, jarring rhymes recalling Byron in *Don Juan*.

The rhythms of *Atta Troll* and *Deutschland* resound in the balladry of Heine's last two collections of verse, *Romanzero* (1851) and *Gedichte 1853 und 1854*; he uses them to exotic, tragic, and at times macabre effect, as in the dance of the slaves in 'Das Sklavenschiff' ('The Slave Ship'). He called the second book of *Romanzero* 'Lamentations' choosing Lazarus as a symbol of his misfortune, and in these moving poems struck a note new to the German lyric, for the good reason, as he said, that no poet had been in such straits before. He chides God with an irreverence that hides the onset of despair. The world may be a vale of tears, full of sin and depravity, but he is loath to leave it; the crude joys of life, food, drink, the accommodating lips of a plump dairy maid, seem sweet in the face of death. No Paradise for him; his wants are more basic:

> Gesundheit nur und Geldzulage
> Verlang ich, Herr! O laß mich froh
> Hinleben noch viel schöne Tage,
> Bei meiner Frau im status quo!

There is a trace of the old self-mockery in the lines:

> O Gott, verkürze meine Qual,
> Damit man mich begrabe;

Du weißt ja, daß ich kein Talent
Zum Martyrtume habe.

but in 'Morphine' it is a latter-day Job we hear, cursing his day and
the night which said, there is a man child conceived:

Gut ist der Schlaf, der Tod ist besser—freilich
Das beste wäre, nie geboren sein.

Heine's poetry is but a fraction of his work; it was through his
prose that he acted as prophet, enlightener-general of his generation,
interpreting France to Germany and Germany to France. He first
turned to prose as an escape from his song-writing; circumstances
then took a hand and turned him into a foreign correspondent,
writing for French and German periodicals or contriving miscellanies
of his own. He had to be readable to live and thus tried to impart a
Gallic gloss to the homespun texture of German prose. In the *West-
minster Review* of 1856, George Eliot paid tribute to his clarity,
precision, and varied rhythms. 'No dreary labyrinthine sentences,'
she wrote, 'in which you find "no end in wandering mazes lost"; no
chains of adjectives in linked harshness long drawn out.' His writing,
as he admitted, was mannered, too persistently epigrammatic, with
strident passages, but he is never dull. His renowned wit is used
more sparingly than might be supposed and varies according to his
purpose; in his treatment of ideas, for example, the friction between
solemn subject and flippant phrase can give polish to a potentially
dull exposition. 'Wit,' he said, 'is only tolerable to me if it rests on a
serious foundation.' His enemies found him tasteless and frivolous;
his friends knew him to be in lively, if not deadly earnest.

His first prose work, *Briefe aus Berlin* (*Letters from Berlin*) was
published in a Rhineland journal in 1822, when Heine was still a
law student. It set a pattern followed in his four volumes of
Reisebilder (*Travel Sketches*, 1826–31). His travels took him to
Munich, Italy, and London, where his sojourn in damp and smoggy
lodgings off the Strand biased him permanently and irrationally, he
later conceded, against Britain. The freshest of these sketches is *Die
Harzreise*, an impressionistic record, with lyrical interludes, of a
journey through the Harz Mountains, starting from his university

town, Göttingen, whose inhabitants he divided into four imperfectly differentiated classes, students, professors, Philistines, and livestock. The travel sketch was a fit outlet for his restless body and mind; he uses it for satire, now playful, now venomous, for romantic pictures of nature, for excursions into politics and ideas, and for confessional outpourings. The moods change quickly, the form is erratic. *Ideen. Das Buch le Grand* (*Ideas. The Book le Grand*) which appeared in the second volume of *Reisebilder*, gets its sub-title from a diminutive, bewhiskered drummer, quartered on the Heines during the French occupation of Düsseldorf, who infected the infant Heine with his hero-worship of Napoleon; starting off as a tale of unrequited love, it merges into an account of Heine's boyhood, records the impact of the French Revolution upon him, and offers an *apologia* for his particular kind of poetry.

Heine's prose writings are liberally bespattered with his personality. As reporter of the French scene, as historian of German ideas, as literary critic, he intrudes himself freely, with all his prejudices and preoccupations, into his work. His prose took strange forms, none stranger than the four volumes of *Der Salon* (1834–40). The title derived from an account of the Paris Salon exhibition of 1831 and the miscellany included a fragmentary novel on the plight of the Jews in sixteenth-century Germany, letters on the French theatre, accounts of erotic adventures, reflections on painting and music, and a discourse on Germanic nature-spirits; for good measure he threw in two collections of verse. The whole of the second volume was taken up with an exposition of German religion and philosophy (*Zur Geschichte der Religion und Philosophie in Deutschland*, 1834). Originally written in French, this was part of Heine's *De l'Allemagne*, his counterblast to the earlier work with the same title by Mme de Staël. In characteristic fashion, he set about correcting Mme de Staël's picture of a land of poets and thinkers, whose spiritualism was a standing reproach to French materialism. Using intellectual tools to whose curious construction Spinoza, Saint-Simon, and Hegel all contributed something, Heine presented the history of German thought in a series of portraits and caricatures. He ended with a dire warning to his French readers. Within the slumbering German giant, explosive intellectual energies were building up. German idealists and natural philosophers might look harmless, but when Kantians turned thoughts into deeds and fanatical Fichteans took up arms, a play would be enacted compared with which the French Revolution would seem an inoffensive idyll. Here we see Heine at his task of 'understanding the present', scanning it for the underlying realities which would shape the future. The role of prophet was only one of many performed by a writer so versatile that each age refashioned him after its own image. Nowadays, the Byronic love-poet has been shelved and the tragic satirist is on display. Like all good satirists, Heine operated from a base of personal ideals, nursing the dream of a heaven upon earth in which hungry humanity would be satisfied and bitterly aware of the difference between things as they are and as they ought to be.

(2)

In the map of German literature, Heine sometimes appears in a region known as 'Young Germany', peopled by a group of writers active between 1830 and the European upheavals of 1848. We have here the odd case of a movement invented by government decree—an edict issued in 1835 by the censorship authorities of the German Confederation, banning 'the works of the literary school known as Young Germany'. There was, it is true, a political organization in Switzerland called Young Germany—it was the period of Mazzini's Young Italy and Disraeli's radical Tory Young England—but neither Heine nor the other writers mentioned in the decree belonged to it, nor were they closely associated with each other; they shared no more than a vaguely liberal outlook. The censor had misread a phrase used by one of them, Ludolf Wienbarg, a young university lecturer, who worked up a series of lectures into a literary manifesto, dedicated to 'Young Germany' in the sense of the modern generation and entitled *Aesthetische Feldzüge* (*Aesthetic Campaigns*). This farrago of moral exhortation and dogma about service to the 'Zeitgeist', the spirit of the age, which now seems innocent enough, gives us a glimpse of the chaotic ideology of the time. Traditional systems of theology, politics, and economics were all under fire; substitutes for religion like Saint-Simonism, invaded Germany from France; strange forms of primitive socialism blossomed, to be derided by Marx and Engels in *Socialism Utopian and Scientific* and *The German Ideology*. Caught up in what is now diminished to an eddy in the whirlpool of nineteenth-century thought, the 'Young Germans' were doubly unfortunate. Champions in their own eyes of modernity and emancipation, they were viewed by their opponents on the Right as subversive doctrinaires and by the radical Left as aimless dilettanti. The *maladie du siècle* which infected their contemporaries elsewhere in Europe afflicted them in the form of 'Zerrissenheit', the feeling of being poised between an alien past and an uncertain future, torn by divided loyalties, but they were incapable of making literary capital of their spiritual conflicts. Lacking genuine passion, they strike literary attitudes, surfeit us with ideas, and starve us of flesh and blood.

Georg Büchner stands apart from the Young German generation by reason of his radicalism. His vision was dispassionate, his heart compassionate, and his political ideas simple to the point of crudity. 'The relation between poor and rich,' he wrote, 'is the only revolutionary element in the world.' The only levers which would heave the German peasantry out of its torpor were, he believed, dire poverty and religious fanaticism: 'Any party which knows how to manipulate these levers is bound to win.' In a phrase recalling Cobbett's doctrine of the full belly, he told Karl Gutzkow: 'Stuff the peasants with food and the revolution will have an apoplectic fit.' He knew next to nothing about the literature of his day and his aesthetic judgements are as radical as his political: 'The lowliest living creature makes a deeper impression than the mere sensation of beauty.' At the time of his death, he was a lecturer in comparative anatomy at the University of Zürich. His inaugural lecture was on the cranial nerves and he was trained to see the skull beneath the skin. The contrast between the natural order in which things exist for their own sake, careless of plans and purposes, and chaotic humanity, ever in search of the meaning behind the suffering, was never far from his mind: 'The slightest quiver of pain, even if it occurs only in an atom, rends creation from top to bottom.'

Büchner died of typhus at the age of twenty-three. In his short life he wrote three plays (*Dantons Tod* (*The Death of Danton*), *Woyzeck*, and *Leonce und Lena*) and a Novelle, *Lenz*, a clinically precise yet moving record, based on a contemporary account, of the mental breakdown of the Sturm und Drang dramatist. In *Dantons Tod* (1835), Büchner anatomized a revolutionary situation. He wrote the play at his father's dissecting table, the manuscript hidden under a pile of anatomical textbooks, when he was under threat of arrest by the Hessian police after a disastrous experiment with underground political activity. The subject is the trial and execution of Georges Jacques Danton at a time when the future of the French Revolution was in the balance and Robespierre was liquidating opponents to right and left of him. We see the revolution in the round, through the eyes of leaders, people, and bourgeoisie; we are taken from the private rooms of the revolutionaries to the tribunals, to the Conciergerie where Danton was imprisoned and to the Place de la Révolution where he was guillotined. Büchner weaves into the action transcripts of speeches made at the time, but his weary, disillusioned anti-hero is a creature of his own imagination. In a scene with his wife, Danton, tormented by the memory of the September massacres, uncovers the doubt and terror behind his public façade. He has dreamt of riding a runaway world over an abyss of nothingness. 'What I did, I had to do,' he tells himself, and puts the blame on whatever has laid upon him 'der Fluch des Muß', the curse of the 'had to'.

His opponent Robespierre is recognizably the sea-green incorruptible of history, yet he too, in a soliloquy, tries to shuffle off responsibility for his actions. Sleepwalkers all, we do no more in life than act out our nightmares. Our feeble bodies execute no more than a fraction of the dark desires and thoughts within us; whether these turn into deeds or not is pure chance; who then has a right to denounce us for what we do? Robespierre in action is a man of principle, adrift like the rest of the revolutionaries on a sea of ideas. We have been living in the company of ideologues, exposed to a torrent of words, to cerebration about the existence or non-existence of God, to impassioned political arguments, only to find that at the end of the road there is no time for rhetoric or heroic gestures: Danton's last words are a reproach to the executioner who tries to stop him embracing his friend Hérault. The last scene is given to Camille Desmoulins' wife. Determined not to survive him, she calls out

'Long live the king!' in the hearing of a passing citizen and is seized by the guard.

Büchner's Danton is a sophisticated and voluble politician whose life ends with a simple gesture of love. His Woyzeck is a simple and inarticulate being whose life ends with a killing—a complex gesture, of which the motives lie deeper than hatred, retribution, or madness. A celebrated murder case of the early nineteenth century provided the material for the play. In 1821 Johann Christian Woyzeck, a barber turned soldier, stabbed to death the woman with whom he had been living. Seven years later he was beheaded in Leipzig, watched by a large crowd which had been denied the spectacle of a public execution for twenty years. His motive appeared to be primitive jealousy, but in the course of the trial doubts about his sanity arose. A prolonged inquiry led to the conclusion that he was, in fact, responsible for his act. His unbalanced state of mind, his delusions, were due to a disorder of the blood caused by his irregular life, his drunkenness and sexual incontinence. The affair aroused much interest in legal circles as a test case of criminal responsibility in insanity. To Woyzeck's executioners, he knew what he was about and was therefore a bad man; to his defenders he was not responsible for what he did and was therefore a madman. The first judgement was an outrage to Büchner's compassion, the second an offence against his common sense—for if Woyzeck was not responsible for his action, who *was* responsible? A conflict of moral principle, still unsolved, underlay the Woyzeck case. Büchner ignores it, preferring to probe the moral tissue in search of the nerve of life embedded in it. Woyzeck is beyond the reach of the ideals propounded by his tormentors. 'There must be something fine about virtue,' he replies to the Captain who urges him to mend his ways, 'but I am only a poor fellow.' The Doctor, who has subjected Woyzeck, in the interests of science, to an exclusive diet of peas, reproaches him for his incontinence and lectures him on free will. 'Man is free,' the Doctor insists, 'in man we see individuality transfigured into freedom.' Woyzeck racks his brains over these impenetrable doctrines. 'You are a good fellow, but you think too much,' is the Captain's verdict. 'There you go, philosophizing again, Woyzeck,' says the Doctor. Enfeebled in body, his mind not so much unhinged as unendurably sensitized by the loss of his one possession, Marie, who betrays him with the potent and handsome drum-major, Woyzeck is beset by terrible visions: fiery images of heavenly judgement, crazy notions that freemasons are burrowing beneath his feet, subterranean voices urging him to kill Marie. Is he mad? We must judge this ourselves from the scene in which the decision to put an end to her is as it were dictated to him. Marie sits at her door. A child begins a song:

> The sun shines bright at Candlemas,
> The corn is fully ripe ...

The other children will have none of it and ask Marie for another song. She refuses, so the Grandmother takes over with a cruel travesty of a fairy tale. 'Once upon a time,' she begins, 'there was a poor child and it had no father or mother, everybody was dead and there was nobody left in the world.' The moon when the child reached it was a piece of rotten wood, the sun a withered sunflower, the stars midges impaled upon the sky. The earth, when she got back to it, was an upturned pot. She sat down and cried and there she still sits alone. It is at this point that Woyzeck abruptly appears and laconically summons Marie to her death.

We do not know how the play was meant to end. It is a fragment —twenty-eight unnumbered scenes, of which the sequence is variable. The intended finale may have been the scene in which the policeman rubs his hands in glee that such a fine murder should have, for once, come his way. To bring the curtain down on this scene is to sharpen the social criticism in the play, to show Woyzeck as a defenceless creature pressurized out of existence by superior forces. Alternatively, the last word can be given to the heartless children who tell Marie's boy that his mother is dead and dance off to view the corpse lying by the pond. This is to see the play as a bleak assertion of the reality of pain and Woyzeck himself as a monument to those who suffer whether deservedly or not. It is the method used by Alban Berg in his opera *Wozzeck*. The effect is desolating: the screw has been given another turn.

Woyzeck (1836) has even less in common with conventional 'drama' than *Dantons Tod*. Powerful feelings and complex moods

are conveyed with a minimum of effort. The dialogue is terse and
robust: Büchner never wastes nor minces a word. Snatches of folk-
song are used with telling effect. He constantly changes key, anticipating the modulations familiar to us in twentieth-century theatre;
he can be blackly humorous and grotesque, ironic, tender, and
even absurd. He is not all unrelieved gloom; in *Leonce und Lena*
(1836), which owes much to Alfred de Musset, the follies of society
and the *maladie du siècle*, melancholy boredom, are made the stuff
of a satirical comedy. Büchner was discovered late but since the end
of the nineteenth century he has never looked like going out of
fashion; indeed theatrical fashions have been hard put to it to keep
up with him.

(3)

Büchner had no contact with the contemporary stage; his plays
were first performed nearly a century after his death. In his day and
for the greater part of the nineteenth century the liveliest centre of
the dramatic arts was Vienna, where all tastes were served. High-
brow drama had its home in the Burgtheater, in which dialect was
taboo, while Austrian popular comedy flourished in the playhouses,
the Theater in der Josefstadt, the Theater in der Leopoldstadt, and
the Theater an der Wien, which had been established to house it.
They provided diverse entertainment: burlesques, parodies, trav-
esties, topical comedies, fairy-tale farces, spectacular shows in which
the devices of the Baroque stage—fireworks, waterworks, and
transformation scenes, were mobilized, in alliance with music, for
the amusement of the spectator. Viennese 'Volkskomödie' lives on
today in Mozart's *Magic Flute*, for which the libretto was written by
the comic dramatist and manager of the Theater an der Wien,
Emanuel Schikaneder. Its heyday was the mid-nineteenth century,
the age of Ferdinand Raimund and Johann Nestroy. Raimund's
'Zauberspiele' and 'Zaubermärchen' transport us to a magical world
in which good and evil spirits battle for the souls of men. He puts
across, through colourful and transparent allegories, a homespun and
charitable philosophy, viewing the failings of mankind with mild
scepticism and gentle humour. After his death in 1836, the Viennese
popular theatre was dominated for twenty years by Nestroy, a

brilliant comic actor, a prolific dramatist, and a satirist of the first rank. The Quodlibets and Couplets which enliven his farces are very different from Raimund's wistful songs. Their background is the money-grubbing Vienna of the early industrial age, a world of shady speculators, not-so-trusty retainers, and not-so-sturdy artisans, among them the ropemaker's apprentice Fabian Strick, a part played by Nestroy himself. In *Die beiden Nachtwandler oder Das Notwendige und das Überflüssige* (*The Two Sleepwalkers or The Necessary and the Superfluous*) he is given a line often quoted as an example of Nestroy's disillusioned cynicism: 'I believe the worst of everyone, even of myself, and so far I have seldom been disappointed.' To see Nestroy's wit as purely destructive is, however, to confuse him with his characters: his satire is not indiscriminate; like Loveless in Vanbrugh's *The Relapse*, he invites us to 'pity those whom Nature abuses, but never those who abuse Nature'.

As a manipulator of the German language Nestroy has few equals. His mind expressed itself most readily in word-play and it is thus not surprising that Ludwig Wittgenstein should have gone to him for the motto of his *Philosophical Investigations*: 'It is the very nature of progress to look greater than it really is.' For Nestroy, truth is elusive, language ambiguous, and thought treacherous. 'The more I plumb the depths of my ideas,' he said, 'the more I plunge into an abyss of contradictions.' He juggles and struggles with ideas in a style, far removed from the crude verbal humour of his predecessors, marked by proliferating comic metaphors and those tart reflections upon experience, of which a quota will be found in all collections of German aphorisms.

Raimund and Nestroy were professional entertainers, their natural element the Viennese theatre. Franz Grillparzer operated on its fringe. He earned his living amid the dusty files of the Hofkammer Archive, a conscientious, if disgruntled, servant of the Habsburg Empire, venting his energies and griefs in the verse tragedies he offered to the fickle public of the Burgtheater. He was drawn to the stage by an inner compulsion, yet at heart, as he confessed in his diary, he loathed it; he cut himself adrift from it after the failure, in 1838, of his only comedy and lived on to 1872, still writing or sketching tragedies. Grillparzer is one of the few major nineteenth-century playwrights before the advent of Ibsen. A Catholic, and an Austrian Catholic to boot, he had a strong sense of a natural order trying to impose itself on the confusion of human affairs and at first sight his plays, sprinkled with prim moral reflections, seem orthodox enough. Nevertheless, he was in his own way an innovator and a realist. His unheroic heroes and heroines foreshadow the end of tragedy as a major genre in European literature. He does not, like Schiller, bid us flex our moral muscles in a spasm of exhilaration, glorying in our spiritual freedom; he intends us to leave the theatre in subdued and reflective mood, pondering our frailty and our helplessness in face of uncontrollable impulse. 'The basic errors of human nature,' he wrote, 'are the truths of poetry.' His verse, at its best, is a transparent flow of words, through which we can see, beneath their actions, the inner life of his characters, the obscure realities hidden in, and from them, by their hearts:

> Von wo der Mensch beginnt, womit er endet,
> Und was für Mächte in der Brust verbirgt,
> Und was für Mächte seine Brust ihm bergen,
> Das ist der Inhalt unsers ernsten Spiels.

Grillparzer made two concessions to dramatic fashion: the Gothic fate-tragedy *Die Ahnfrau* (*The Ancestress*) and the fairy-tale play *Der Traum ein Leben* (*A Life within the Compass of a Dream*). Otherwise he took his subjects from Greek legend and the past of Austria, Hungary, Bohemia, and Spain. His most elaborate historical play, *König Ottokars Glück und Ende* (1825), dealt with the rise and fall of the Bohemian king whose defeat by Rudolph the First established the greatness of the House of Habsburg. It had a thirteenth-century setting, but the theme—'vaulting ambition which o'erleaps itself' and the corrupting influence of power—was topical, for it was written a few years after the death of a more recent upstart and disturber of the peace, Napoleon. In his three Greek tragedies, *Sappho* (1818), the trilogy *Das goldene Vließ* (*The Golden Fleece*, 1820), and his dramatization of the Hero and Leander story *Des Meeres und der Liebe Wellen* (*The Waves of Love and of the Sea*, 1831), he showed the impact of love upon three women—Sappho, a poetess and priestess, Hero, a virgin priestess of Aphrodite, and

Medea, a barbaric sorceress—ill constituted, or badly placed by circumstance, to withstand it. Grillparzer strips these legendary figures of their grandeur and cuts them down to size. His Sappho steps down from her proper sphere, falls in love with an unsophisticated youth, loses him to her young serving woman, and leaps to her death from a cliff in Lesbos. The play can be taken as a parable about the cleavage between art and life, but Grillparzer, irritated because people kept looking for ideas in his plays, offered a less elaborate explanation. There was he conceded, an idea in *Sappho*, the kind of idea which might have occurred to any Viennese cabdriver: 'Gleich und Gleich gesellt sich gern'—like attracts like. The idea is humdrum, the projection of it subtle. Sappho is a complex being and the motives for her suicide are far from simple. Her end, if dignified, is anything but sublime. She dies, to judge from her final prayer to the Gods, of emotional and moral exhaustion:

> Zu schwach fühl ich mich, länger noch zu kämpfen,
> Gebt mir den Sieg, erlasset mir den Kampf!

Grillparzer came across an observation by Rousseau which could well, he thought, serve as a motto for *Medea*, the final play in the Golden Fleece trilogy: 'L'on a remarqué que la plupart des hommes sont dans le cours de leur vie souvent dissemblables à eux-mêmes et semblent se transformer en des hommes tout différents.' The instability of our personality, the difficulty of being true to a self that is always changing—these are among the themes of *Medea*. The story of Jason and his outlandish wife, ending in Medea's murder of her children, becomes the bleak chronicle of a disastrous marriage, of a man and woman entangled in their past, who outgrow each other and the romantic illusions of their youth and live on to see revulsion take the place of love.

'A high intellect'—this was Byron's judgement of Grillparzer, after reading an Italian translation of *Sappho*. It is misleading, for Grillparzer was not an intellectual writer and shared with Yeats the view that 'philosophy would clip an angel's wings'; he provides material for thought without making thought the material of his plays. He exhibits an engaging mixture of assurance and diffidence; he took on tasks which would have daunted a consortium of Racine and Shakespeare and was then plagued by doubts about his capacity to fulfil them; he combined an exalted view of art with a rueful awareness of its absurdity. He keeps well out of sight behind his characters but we catch a glimpse of him in his story *Der arme Spielmann* (*The Poor Fiddler*), part caricature, part idealized self-portrait, which we shall meet with a little later.

Grillparzer is little known outside the German-speaking world. The trouble lies partly in his verse, which travels badly across language frontiers and partly in the subdued quality of his writings; had he been a shade more strident, we would hear him more clearly today.

(4)

Grillparzer's counterpart in poetry was Eduard Mörike; the tone of their work is similar, they were akin in their hatred of meretricious writing and in their remoteness from the ideological fashions of their time. Mörike, however, has reached a wide public on the carrier wave of song. His poetry has been set to music by over three hundred composers, the most faithful interpreter among them being Hugo Wolf. The settings in Wolf's *Mörike-Liederbuch* of 1888 not only recapture the mood of the poems but follow accurately in the vocal line Mörike's rhythms and speech melodies. The composer's favourite among Mörike's poems is 'Das verlassene Mägdlein', the lament of a jilted servant-girl:

> Früh, wann die Hähne krähn,
> Eh die Sternlein verschwinden,
> Muß ich am Herde stehn,
> Muß Feuer zünden.

> Schön ist der Flammen Schein,
> Es springen die Funken,
> Ich schaue so drein,
> In Leid versunken.

> Plötzlich, da kommt es mir,
> Treuloser Knabe,
> Daß ich die Nacht von dir
> Geträumet habe.

Träne auf Träne dann
Stürzet hernieder;
So kommt der Tag heran—
O ging' er wieder!

'Das verlassene Mägdlein' is as good an example as any of Mörike
working the rich vein of folk-song opened up by his predecessors.
It is not, however, typical of his love poetry. Pathos and sweetness
were not to his taste—he disliked, for example, Chamisso's *Frauen-
Liebe und Leben*—and at times, as in 'Erstes Liebeslied eines Mäd-
chens ('A Girl's First Love-Song'), strikes an unromantic note of
frank sexuality. It would, indeed, be hard to cite a typical Mörike
poem. He does not repeat himself and when he fulfils our expectations, he does so like a good composer, in an unexpected way. His
inventiveness is tireless but not capricious; if he rings the changes
on Germanic and classical verse forms, it is because he is intent on
saying what he has to say in the right way. 'Nur nichts forciren'
(roughly translated 'Never force the pace') was his rule of thumb.
By keeping within his natural limits he achieves a poise which sets
him apart from the ruck of nineteenth-century German poets; his
serious verse is sombre, but avoids synthetic gloom; his light verse,
which included some nonsense poetry, is whimsical but never arch;
he can write idyllic verse without sentimentalizing Nature. The best
known of his idylls, 'Der alte Turmhahn', shows his talent for
making good poetry out of unpromising subject-matter. The old
weathercock of the title was salvaged by Mörike when the spire
of his church in the Swabian village of Cleversulzbach was repaired
in 1840. Retired, after a century of service, to the top of a stove, the
weathercock surveys the weekly round and common tasks of the
parsonage and ruminates upon his happy lot. A decorous and complacent bird—but only human, after all, for he has twinges of vanity
and venturesome urges unseemly in so venerable a servant of
the church and has to remind himself sharply to keep his mind on
higher things. 'Der alte Turmhahn' is written in doggerel, enlivened
by outrageous rhymes, but in his graver verse Mörike exploits the
tonal richness of German and the opportunities it offers of convey-
ing fine shades of mood. The poem 'Im Frühling' finds him sitting
on a hillside in spring, emitting, like one of those Aeolian harps of

which he was fond, indeterminate melodies, but determined, as the last verse shows, to record them precisely:

> Ich denke dies und denke das,
> Ich sehne mich und weiß nicht recht, nach was:
> Halb ist es Lust, halb ist es Klage;
> Mein Herz, o sage,
> Was webst du für Erinnerung
> In golden grüner Zweige Dämmerung!—
> Alte unnennbare Tage!

He had learnt in the hard school of Greek literature that it is not enough to have beautiful thoughts and fine feelings; they need body if they are to be recognizable as art. And so even his most delicate poems, like 'Septembermorgen' are never flimsy.

> Im Nebel ruhet noch die Welt,
> Noch träumen Wald und Wiesen:
> Bald siehst du, wenn der Schleier fällt,
> Den blauen Himmel unverstellt,
> Herbstkräftig die gedämpfte Welt
> In warmem Golde fließen.

It is a nebulous poem in the sense that it is about the dissipation of autumn mists by the rising sun, but there is nothing vague about it. The words stand out from the page as if embossed.

Mörike spent seventeen years of his life as an itinerant curate and, later, pastor in his native Swabia. A hypochondriac and deficient in zeal, he was induced to retire at the age of thirty-nine and in later life taught German literature, for one hour a week, to the daughters of gentlefolk in an academy in Stuttgart. In what he called his 'noli-me-tangere' past, he entangled himself with a Swiss barmaid of vagrant habits, mysterious origins, and dubious morality and contracted, in his forties, an uneasy union with a colonel's daughter. Modest honours, an honorary professorship, the Order of Maximilian, came his way and he died unobtrusively in 1875. He was religious, but in an unorthodox mode. 'In my better moments,' he wrote to his sister, 'I have a firm and distinct belief that Providence is subjecting me to a well-meant but somewhat tiring educational process.' We hear him at his devotions in the poem entitled 'Gebet':

Herr! schicke, was du willt,
Ein Liebes oder Leides;
Ich bin vergnügt, daß beides
Aus deinen Händen quillt.

Wollest mit Freuden
Und wollest mit Leiden
Mich nicht überschütten!
Doch in der Mitten
Liegt holdes Bescheiden.

'Thy will be done,' is the burden of his prayer, 'but not to excess.'
He had a taste for the occult and when pressed to cut down the
supernatural element in his novel *Maler Nolten* (*Nolten the Painter*)
he complained: 'I wanted to build a dark room and now they insist
that I put in a window.' In his 'better moments' he found consolation
in Nature. At other times, he sensed a threat from mysterious forces
operating behind the sights, sounds, and colours of the world around
him and was afflicted by that 'unbekanntes Wehe', the indefinable
unease which informs many of his poems. He strikes us as a man
who believed in God, but who was uncertain of His benevolence.

(5)

Mörike will be encountered later as a story-teller, in company with
two other writers, Theodor Storm and Annette von Droste-Hülshoff,
who are notable both for their poetry and their prose. Storm was a
native of Schleswig-Holstein and his temperament seems to have
been penetrated by the grey mists of the North Sea. In his first story,
Immensee, written in 1849 when he was still in his early thirties, he
assumed the guise of an old man, looking back upon the lost love
of his youth, and struck a note of mournful resignation which echoes
in the poems he published three years later. To read them is to be
reminded of Verlaine's comment on Tennyson's *In Memoriam*:
'When he should have been broken-hearted, he had many reminis-
cences.' Storm aimed at simplicity and a direct appeal to the heart,
but spoilt the effect of many a good poem by lapses into bathos. His
talent matured slowly and he is at his best in his later prose works.
Annette von Droste-Hülshoff, whose *Gedichte* appeared in the same

year, 1838, as Mörike's, is marked by the intensity of her vision, whether directed outwards at her native Westphalian countryside or inwards, to record the conflict between her critical understanding and her Catholic faith. She ranks as Germany's greatest poetess, yet is not altogether at ease in her lyrical and religious verse. Torn between the urge to express her most intimate feelings and a reluctance to expose them to public view, she created a distinctive idiom, harsh in tone and gritty in texture. Her one adventure into prose fiction, *Die Judenbuche* (*The Jew's Beech*) is so good as to suggest that she would have done well to choose, like her contemporaries the Brontë sisters, the novel or the short story as her medium. The juxtaposition of this earnest and high-minded writer and the outstanding comic poet of the century, incongruous as it doubtless seems, may serve as a reminder that poets can be serious in very different modes.

Wilhelm Busch became famous through his 'Bildergeschichten' —pictorial series anticipating the comic strip—and his illustrated tales in verse. His work depends for its effect, more than, for example, Edward Lear's *Book of Nonsense*, on the marriage of drawing and text, but like Lear he hit upon a memorable kind of terse verse, so that many of his rhymes have become household words in Germany. He was a brilliant draughtsman, economical of line, adept at portraying people and animals in grotesque movement. He studied painting in Antwerp and Munich and in 1859 began to contribute caricatures to the comic weekly *Fliegende Blätter*, adding captions later because, as he said, 'you can't quote pictures'. In 1865 he produced the series which fixed his reputation inside and outside Germany—*Max und Moritz*, 'the story of two young rascals in seven escapades', illustrated with coloured woodcuts. It is a poor measure of his range and quality. Although children figure often in his work, his satire was chiefly directed at their elders, at their malice, hypocrisy, and credulity. In a late prose work, *Eduards Traum* (*Edward's Dream*), he surveyed the dehumanized world of Wilhelmine Germany through the eyes of a man who dreams he has changed into a mathematical point and in *Kritik des Herzens* (*Critique of the Heart*), the best of his three volumes of unillustrated verse, he revealed himself as a sharp-eyed and a sharp-tongued moralist.

The English counterpart of Max and Moritz will be found in Hilaire Belloc's *Cautionary Tales for Children*, in characters like 'Matilda, who told lies and was burnt to death' or 'Henry King, who chewed pieces of string and was early cut off in dreadful agonies'. Their common ancestor was Struwwelpeter, the boy who let his hair and nails grow wild. Struwwelpeter first appeared in 1848, in a book entitled *Lustige Geschichten und drollige Bilder für Kinder von 3-6 Jahren* (*Merry Tales and Droll Pictures for Children aged 3 to 6*), illustrated by coloured lithographs and intended by the author, Heinrich Hoffmann, a Frankfurt doctor, as a Christmas present for his four-year-old son. Despite the family likeness, Struwwelpeter, Fidgety Phil, Johnny Head-in-Air, and Airborne Robert are much more innocent than Max and Moritz; Hoffmann's children, apart from Cruel Frederick, are naughty; Busch's are noxious. Specialists in the spiteful practical joke, they come to a deservedly bad end; ground up into chicken feed, and eaten by the miller's geese, they perish unwept, if not unsung.

Busch's most popular cautionary tale for grown-ups was *Die fromme Helene* (*Pious Helen*, 1872)—a title modelled on Offenbach's operetta, *La Belle Hélène*. We first meet Helene as an ill-behaved little girl, heedless of the sound advice given her by her guardians, self-righteous Uncle Nolte and his virtuous wife. She gives her heart to Cousin Franz, but settles for G. J. C. Schmock, one of Busch's archetypal German 'Kleinbürger'. As the union is fruitless, she goes on a pilgrimage and by the grace of God and the assistance of Cousin Franz produces twins. A double disaster follows: Schmock chokes to death on a fish-bone and Franz is brained by a jealous serving-man. Helene burns her frippery, dons sober black, and takes to penitence and drink. Overturning a lamp, she is burnt to a cinder and is carried off to the underworld, after her Good Genius has battled unsuccessfully for her soul with the Devil. The moral of this mordant *Frauen-Liebe und Leben* is drawn by Uncle Nolte:

> Das Gute—dieser Satz steht fest—
> Ist stets das Böse, was man läßt!

The dictum: What's Good, but Evil left undone? has fixed Busch's reputation as a pessimist. It is no surprise to find it in a distorted echo of St. Paul's 'The good I would I do not; but the evil which I would not that I do', for the New Testament was a regular item in Busch's spiritual diet, which included St. Augustine, Schopenhauer, and Darwin. There is no denying his bleak view of humanity. A generation before Freud, he exploded the myth of childish innocence and created a race of ruthless little monsters. In the knives, forks, and scissors which fill his drawings we can descry symbols, and in his umbrellas, actual agents of castration; he presents life as a battlefield and marriage as guerrilla warfare. Busch is not to everybody's taste; he has been accused of playing upon our 'Schadenfreude', our malicious delight in the misfortunes of others, even of sadism. To judge him thus is to miss the deeply sceptical but nevertheless humane mind concealed by the drastic humour. He is unsparing of our illusions and aware at the same time of the limitations of our reason; we see through a glass darkly and if we are a bad lot, we are, after all, no worse than we ought to be.

(6)

In the mid-nineteenth century, poetry and drama were swamped by the flood of fiction which poured, at the rate of over a thousand novels and tales a year, from the German printing presses. Most of them are now lost in the limbo of forgotten books and among the survivors, the preponderant type is the 'Novelle', the long short story or miniature novel, a form apt to curb the native bent for luxuriant fancy and rambling construction. The best of these 'Novellen' were included in an anthology, entitled *Deutsche Erzähler* made early in the present century by Hugo von Hofmannsthal, who described his 'German Story-tellers' as voices from a more wholesome world than his own; he loved their spirituality, that awareness of the mystery beneath the surface of things lacking in their hither-worldly French contemporaries; so much a part of him were their stories that he needed no other aid than memory in the business of selection. For the outsider, with a different cultural heritage, their appeal is necessarily more limited. Many good tales of rural life in Germany, Austria, or Switzerland, for example, are embedded, to the point of inaccessibility, in the remote past of a particular region. There are, however, three memorable exceptions:

Jeremias Gotthelf's *Die schwarze Spinne* (*The Black Spider*, 1842), Annette von Droste-Hülshoff's *Die Judenbuche* (*The Jew's Beech*, 1842), and Theodor Storm's *Der Schimmelreiter* (*The Rider on the White Horse*, 1888). In *Die Schwarze Spinne*, a description of a christening feast in a Bernese village serves as framework for an allegory, woven out of folk-memories of an ancient pestilence, of the evil dormant even in the most secure communities. Both *Der Schimmelreiter* and *Die Judenbuche* recount rustic tragedies set in the eighteenth century, the one located in the highlands of Westphalia, the other on the coast of North Friesland, played out among peasant communities whose ingrained paganism is overlaid by a veneer of Christianity. Both chronicle the lives of men, moulded by their surroundings yet set apart from their fellows by exceptional qualities of mind and temperament, who are driven by the play of circumstances to self-destruction.

The hero of *Die Judenbuche*, Friedrich Mergel, grows up in an isolated village in the Teutoburger Forest among tough and enterprising peasants adept at the illegal felling of timber. He is the only son of a superannuated village beauty and a drunken small farmer, linked in a disastrous marriage. In early childhood, he loses his father, who achieves immortality as the local ghost, haunting the wood in which his corpse was found, and is entrusted to the care of a disreputable uncle. A good workman, handsome, with a reputation as the local dandy, he is prone both to fits of moody withdrawal and bouts of self-display. His love of showing off is his downfall: he bilks a Jewish dealer from whom he has acquired a silver watch, is exposed and humiliated at a wedding feast, bludgeons the Jew to death, and buries him beneath a beech tree. The Jews of the neighbourhood buy the tree, to ensure that it will never be felled, and carve on it in Hebrew characters the inscription: 'If you come near this place, you will suffer the same fate as you dealt to me.' Friedrich escapes abroad, spends years in Turkish slavery, returns to the scene of his crime, hangs himself from a branch of the Jew's beech, and is ingloriously buried in the knacker's yard. An improbable tale, it may be thought, but it is substantially true—the source was the account of a celebrated murder case reconstructed by Droste's uncle from the family archives—and was intended in part as a realistic and unflattering picture of the *mores* of the West-phalian peasantry. But it is more than a period murder story. It appeared about the same time as *Wuthering Heights* and deals, as Charlotte Brontë said of her sister's novel, with 'those tragic and terrible traits of which, in listening to the secret annals of every rude vicinage, the memory is sometimes compelled to receive the impress'. Where Droste embellishes her source—with the invention of a tatterdemalion double for Friedrich, with ambiguities and snatches of conversation in the modern manner, leading nowhere but fraught with impending disaster—it is less to keep us guessing than to stress the limits of our understanding of human destiny. It is the most charitable of thrillers.

Der Schimmelreiter is a much chillier tale. It was Storm's last Novelle, written in 1888, the year of his death, and uses folk-memor-ies of ancient inundations on the Schleswig-Holstein coast as a projection of his vision of death as a black tide ever threatening to engulf him. Hauke Haien, the central figure, is a dikemaster, the son and son-in-law of dikemasters, in features, build, and temperament typical of the lowland farmers among whom he lives yet isolated from them by reason of his superior brains, ambition, and drive. Obsessed with the project of a new dike, he pushes through his plan in face of local jealousy and opposition, but neglects, with fatal consequences, to strengthen an old, adjoining dike. In the great storm of 1783, 'when all the mighty floods were out ... and all the world was in the sea', the old dike is breached, his wife and daughter perish, and Hauke Haien ends his life by plunging, astride his white horse, into the floodwaters. His own dike survives the storm and he himself lives on in popular imagination as a spectral rider, an omen of impending danger from the sea. There is nothing subtle about *Der Schimmelreiter*; the conclusion is foregone, the final catastrophe a storm to end all storms; Hauke Haien's only child is predictably simple-minded; the sorry nag which he gets from a sinister gipsy turns, as might be expected, into the fieriest of steeds. But if we dis-count the period trappings, we are faced with a moving fable on the theme of human endeavour, written by a man who had little to learn about the malevolence of Nature.

For Jeremias Gotthelf (the pen-name of the Swiss pastor Albert

Bitzius), natural catastrophe and moral corruption were alike works of the Devil who would, if sinfulness or shiftlessness gave him an opening, loose anarchy upon the world. This is the moral of the tale told by the grandfather to the guests at the christening feast in *Die schwarze Spinne*. Their forbears, set a superhuman task by their tyrannous overlords, turned to the Devil for help and cheated him of his due, an unbaptized child; he afflicted them with recurrent plagues of venomous black spiders whose monstrous progenitor, thanks to successive acts of self-sacrifice, was at last immured in the door-jamb of the house in which the story is told. Gotthelf considered his novels and tales of peasant life an extension of his cure of souls, a special kind of sermonizing, and denied them the title of works of art. Despite his disclaimer, he reveals himself in *Die schwarze Spinne* as an artificer of remarkable cunning. He interlocks the legend with a realistic account of a sedate and prosperous community of farmers whose life, well ordered by usage and ritual, seems beyond reach of danger and yet is always menaced by the disruptive forces pent up in their hearts. The story is written in robust prose with a range of tone stretching from the colloquial to the rhetorical, designed to make a powerful impact on the reader. To read it today is to perceive how much modern writers have lost through their emancipation from moral and literary conventions. Simplicity of purpose, clear-cut beliefs, and reliance on well-tried techniques are clearly no handicap to the story-teller—provided, of course, that he has Gotthelf's broad understanding of human behaviour, gift of narrative, and complete control of his medium.

Gotthelf, Storm, and Annette von Droste-Hülshoff address themselves to the generality of mankind. Two of their contemporaries, the Austrian Adalbert Stifter and the Swiss Conrad Ferdinand Meyer, seem by contrast to write for a particular kind of reader. Both were specialists in the Novelle, painstaking craftsmen who in an earlier or later age might have found some direct way of expressing their private tensions and torments. As it was, they were born out of time and induced, partly by convention, partly by inclination, to put a well-nigh impenetrable screen between themselves and their public. Stifter's measured, stylized prose is not for the impatient reader. In his *Studien* (*Studies*) and his stories of children, *Bunte Steine* (*Stones of Many Colours*) the pulse of narrative is weak; in his 'Bildungs-roman' *Der Nachsommer* (*Indian Summer*, 1857) it is almost imperceptible. Believing with William Blake that every minute particular is holy, he leads us through a maze of detail, describing natural and man-made things with equal care, to the abstract centre of his world—his ideal of perfection and unpretentious virtue. It needs a discerning eye to detect the anxiety and despair behind the order and harmony which he tried to manifest through the manner and content of his stories. Compared with Stifter, Meyer is some-thing of a grandee. Not for him the search for true greatness in petty things; his taste is for the grandiose. Led to write Novellen, he tells us, by the contemplation of the monumental art of Michelangelo, he favours, in the way of subject matter, great figures from the past. He had an obsessive interest in Thomas Becket and in *Der Heilige* (*The Saint*), written in 1880, he set about unravelling the mystery of Becket's martyrdom (or was it suicide?) with such calculated ambiguity and elaborate irony that the Beckets of Anouilh and Eliot seem, by comparison, to be transparently simple. Meyer's Becket is unique in having a daughter, begotten of a Moorish mother, who is seduced by King Henry and murdered at the behest of Queen Eleanor. We might take her for the cause of Becket's vengefulness (he is the most sinful of saints) were it not that her name, Grace, is pregnant with uncertain meaning. Intent, if we are to believe him, on enlightening us, he ends by baffling us. Is the story an attack on medieval credulity or a Christian parable of crime and punishment? There is nothing unclear, however, about Meyer's style. Critical of the laziness of German prose, he affected sharpness of line, graphic effects, and a disciplined form, attributed by some to French in-fluence and by his compatriot, Gottfried Keller, to the fact that he had little to say. 'I use the historical Novelle,' Meyer wrote, 'purely and simply as a repository for my personal feelings and experiences. I prefer it to the topical novel because it masks me more effectively.' The mask was, if anything, too effective; to get the most out of Meyer's stories we need to be privy to the intimate desires and fantasies which he was at such pains to conceal.

Two of the best Novellen of the period were written not by specialists in the genre but by a poet and a dramatist. Mörike's

Mozart auf der Reise nach Prag (*Mozart on the way to Prague*, 1856) and Grillparzer's *Der arme Spielmann* (*The Poor Fiddler*, 1848) were written with such clarity and delicacy, in a key somewhere between the touching and the absurd, that they are as fresh today as when they were writen over a century ago. Each has an Austrian setting and each has to do with a musician, the one a genius, the other ludicrously inept. The narrator of *Der arme Spielmann*, strolling through the Brigittenau in Vienna during the July fair of 1830, comes across an elderly busker, scraping away, unconcerned at his lack of audience or profit, at a battered fiddle, producing from a sheet of music propped up on a portable stand a cacophonous sequence of disconnected notes. Asked for his life story by the narrator, who had never encountered such an odd combination of clumsiness and artistic zeal, the fiddler insists that he has none—all sorts of things had happened to him, of course, but nothing in particular. Pressed for details, he recounts a succession of lamentable failures; he was despised by his father, done out of his inheritance by a confidence trickster, and lost, to an unromantic butcher, the uncomely, hard-headed but soft-hearted shop-girl to whom he was attached. She left him in no doubt about his failings. He was too gullible, too impractical, too indiscriminately courteous—he was polite, she grumbled, to everybody; above all, he had no instinct for self-preservation. The manner of his death, recounted in an epilogue to the story, confirms her diagnosis. During the great flood of 1830, he wades, considerate to the end, into a cellar to salvage his landlord's petty cash and rate book and dies of pneumonia. A wasted life, it might be thought—and yet a rich and enviable one, for Grillparzer's anti-hero is a serene and a lovable man: his old flame, Barbara, names her son Jakob after him and preserves his fiddle as a kind of holy relic. His existence is bare—he shares an attic with two artisans, separating his tidy domain from theirs by an equatorial chalk line—but he is, as far as any man can be, an island unto himself. His life is given meaning by the very activity at which he is least competent—his music-making. Dragging out the chords, skating over the discords, playing *lentissimo* the tricky passages which he is too conscientious to skip, he creates an apparently hellish noise. But there is method in his madness. 'They play Wolfgang Amadeus Mozart,

they play Sebastian Bach,' he says, 'but nobody ever plays God.'
Happily indifferent to the gap between sublime aspiration and
grotesque execution, he acts out through his music his faith that

> From harmony, from heavenly harmony,
> This universal frame began.

A more exalted musician comes to life in *Mozart auf der Reise
nach Prag*. The story was Mörike's tribute to a composer whom he
regarded as supreme and to whom he was perfectly attuned; he took
infinite trouble with it (demanding a correspondingly high price
from his publisher) and finished it in 1856, in time for the centenary
of Mozart's birth. His character sketch, as he called it, is built around
a core of freely invented situations. Accompanied by his wife
Konstanze, Mozart travels to Prague in the autumn of 1787 for the
first performance of *Don Giovanni*, stops at a village on the
Bohemian border, and strays into the garden of Count von Schinz-
berg. In a fit of abstraction he plucks an orange from a tree intended
as a presentation to the Count's niece, Eugenie, on the occasion of
her betrothal. A felicitous gaffe, for the outcome is that Mozart and
Konstanze spend the evening with the Count and his family and
share in the betrothal celebrations. There is much making of music,
excerpts from *Don Giovanni* are performed, Mozart tells how he
composed the finale of the opera, the dreadful *dibattimento* between
the Don and the Commendatore's ghost, and Konstanze illustrates
her husband's amiable eccentricity by an episode from his life in
Vienna. The next morning they go on their way in a carriage presented to them by the Count. Using these simple subjects, developed
through revealing conversations and pointed details, linked by subtle
transitions, Mörike re-creates for us the reality of Mozart and his
music. Not that he claims to give us the whole of Mozart; we see him
in carefree mood, making light of the drudgery, professional
jealousies, and domestic confusion which he has left behind in
Vienna. But we are given glimpses of a man whose every pleasure
was seasoned with grief and chagrin, full of self-distrust, prodigal of
his energies, with a precarious hold on life. Melancholy undertones
are audible in the brilliant section on *Don Giovanni*, for Mörike the
greatest of all operas but too full for him of intimate associations to

be bearable, and are clearly sounded in the *coda* with which the story ends. After Mozart's departure, Eugenie has a foreboding of his early death. Her family scoff at her fears but her instinct did not deceive her. A few years later, shortly after his last visit to Prague, Mozart was dead, at the age of thirty-four. Mörike is content to leave us with no more than an intimation of mortality, in the form of a poem, palmed off on us as an old Bohemian folk-song, which drops out of a pile of music left on the piano on which Mozart has performed:

> Ein Tännlein grünet wo,
> Wer weiß, im Walde;
> Ein Rosenstrauch, wer sagt,
> In welchem Garten?
> Sie sind erlesen schon,
> Denk' es, o Seele,
> Auf deinem Grab zu wurzeln
> Und zu wachsen.
>
> Zwei schwarze Rößlein weiden
> Auf der Wiese,
> Sie kehren heim zur Stadt
> In muntern Sprüngen.
> Sie werden schrittweis gehn
> Mit deiner Leiche;
> Vielleicht, vielleicht noch eh'
> An ihren Hufen
> Das Eisen los wird,
> Das ich blitzen sehe!

(7)

A good German Novelle is like a good piece of music; we feel the writer to be firmly in control, whereas in the novel we often sense him struggling with his medium. This was not for lack of thought about it; prose writers and philosophers alike pondered the problem of what a novel ought to be, devising theories of which the most characteristic was Arthur Schopenhauer's. Writing in 1851, he judged the quality of a novel by the preponderance in it of inner over outer life; it was not the novelist's task, he argued, to narrate great events, but to make small ones interesting. Many German, Swiss, and Austrian writers followed this prescription and thus we perceive behind their novels, however various the settings and characters, much the same kind of man at work. He is deeply serious, but not without whimsicality and irony. Operating from a humanist pulpit rather than from a writing desk, he defends ideals and values in face of materialism and social instability. He would like to be popular, if only popularity could be reconciled with literary excellence. His prefaces, directed to the new mass public, are no longer the letters of introduction addressed by his eighteenth-century predecessors to well-tried friends; they resemble passports, soliciting fair treatment in a hostile land. His models are *Wilhelm Meister* and *Tristram Shandy*; he is his own hero, his subject is his own view of life. Yet he aspires to a realistic portrayal of society and knows his Dickens, only to feel, like Thackeray, that 'there is no writing against such power as this—one has no chance'. Lacking the material provided by London and Paris, he chronicles the life of the countryside, the village, and the small town; he does so skilfully and lovingly but generates a localized interest and is seldom read abroad. While this composite portrait does little justice to a major novelist like Theodor Fontane, it is a truer likeness of undistinguished but significant writers like Karl Immermann and Gustav Freytag. Immermann, a lawyer by profession and later director of the Düsseldorf theatre, observed with a satirical, yet sentimental eye, the two decades following the Napoleonic Wars. Freytag, a Silesian journalist, dramatist, and novelist, shows us a later stage in the transition from the old order to the new, the period after the revolution of 1848. Both aim at period novels depicting German society and in particular the tension between the land-owning nobility and the industrial and commercial *arrivistes*; both end by conjuring up the familiar figure of the 'Zeitgeist', the spirit of the age.

There is no stranger embodiment of the 'Zeitgeist' than the hero of Immermann's *Münchhausen. Eine Geschichte in Arabesken* (*Münchhausen. A Story in Arabesques*, 1838). Two stories with many ramifications are entwined in arabesque patterns in *Münchhausen*. The first is a satire which leaves hardly any of the follies and pretensions of the age untouched. The second is part love story, part realistic chronicle of rural life in Westphalia, and is used by Immermann to expound his own values and ideals. The archetypal liar who is the vehicle for his satire was based on a real original, an eighteenth-century Hanoverian nobleman notorious for tall stories of his adventures as a campaigner against the Turks in Russian service. He entered European literature by way of *Baron Münchhausen's Narrative of his Marvellous Travels and Campaigns in Russia*, which was published in London in 1785, written in collaboration with assorted hacks by Rudolf Erich Raspe, an unfrocked academic and swindler who had taken refuge in England. His booklet had many sequels, some illustrated by Rowlandson and Cruikshank, and made its way to Germany in a free translation by the Sturm-und-Drang poet Bürger.

Immermann's Münchhausen is a ludicrous, pitiful, yet frightening figure, with his piercing blue eyes and his habit, when overwrought, of turning green instead of red, due to a disturbance of his body chemistry. Without any guiding principles, he lives from hand to mouth—'The whole of life is an impromptu', he declares. Lacking any other outlet for his talents, he has become a liar of heroic proportions. His trouble is that he is all head—he is a member of almost all learned societies—and lacks a heart. Tapping his breast, he echoes the Speaker's words in Ecclesiastes: 'Emptiness, emptiness, all is empty!' At once a Quixotic visionary and a fraud, he has a scheme for converting air into bricks—an idea borrowed by Immermann from *Gulliver's Travels*. The Universal Artist whom Gulliver, while on a visit to the Academy of Lagoda, sees engaged on a process for 'condensing air into a dry tangible substance' is a disinterested, if crackbrained, scientist; the less scrupulous Münchhausen has floated a company—the Air Condensation Company—for the commercial exploitation of the discovery, or more probably of the shareholders. On a scientific journey in connection with this project, Münchhausen, accompanied by his Sancho Panza, Karl Buttervogel, arrives at the tumbledown castle of Schnick-Schnack-Schnurr and thus enters a world recalling Thomas Love Peacock's contemporaneous satire *Crotchet Castle*. That folly and fraudulence know no frontiers is apparent from the kinship between Immermann's monomaniacs and cranks and Peacock's 'perfectibilians, deteriorationists, status-quoists, transcendentalists, theorists in all sciences, morbid visionaries and romantic enthusiasts'. Münchhausen had the making of a great comic character but Immermann, with his limited inventiveness, was no match for him; he disappears inexplicably two-thirds of the way through the book, with only a hint that he finally settled down as a solid citizen in south Germany. The other part of *Münchhausen*, which is readily detachable from the body of the novel, is still read today under the title of *Der Oberhof* (*The Top Farm*); the satire, capricious in form and full of impenetrable allusions, has dwindled to a curiosity of literature. *Münchhausen* is a complex novel, but its message is simple: the cure for the 'moral seasickness' and intellectual chaos of the age must be sought in right feeling, in the heart rather than the head. Heir to a burdensome past and undisturbed by the Utopian dreams of his more radical contemporaries, he nevertheless clung to traditional values and ways of life. His *Münchhausen* is a defence of the heart as the last refuge of a divided mind.

Freytag's most striking quality was his single-mindedness; he saw the social tensions of his time with the unclouded, if blinkered eyes of a German liberal nationalist. His *Soll und Haben* (*Debit and Credit*) was a success from the moment of its publication in 1855 and has remained to this day one of the outstanding best-sellers among German novels. It is a business-like 'Bildungsroman'; the hero is Anton Wohlfahrt (the name means 'Welfare'), a young provincial of modest origins who works his way up in the world of commerce and finishes as a partner in his employer's export–import firm. He and his 'Principal' embody the Victorian virtues of industry, probity, and orderliness, here presented as essentially German middle-class attributes capable of forming, by extension, the ethical core of a new Germany. Citadel of rectitude though he is, Anton is not impregnable; he is temporarily seduced from his true path by the dazzling life-style of his social superiors, represented by Baron von Rothsattel and his family. Rothsattel, an aristocratic landowner, is an anachronism in the new industrial age; his foray into the world of business ends in disaster and dishonour, due to his vanity, class prejudices, and general incompetence. The agent of his ruin is an upstart Jewish financier, a symbol of the lure of dishonest gain rather than an expression of Freytag's anti-Semitism. The Jewish characters in the novel are not alone in being judged by the degree to which they can be absorbed into Freytag's scheme of things. Even his hero Anton is so judged; dullish and humourless, he cuts a Pooter-like figure compared with the ideal character, Fritz von Fink. Fink, part shrewd business operator, part dashing cavalry officer, comes into his own in the second half of the story, in which a field of action ampler than the counting-house and warehouse is opened up. The scene is Prussian Poland, a region peopled by feckless Slavonic peasants and nobles, bereft of a middle class and ripe for development by sturdy German settlers like Anton, who has become bailiff of an estate acquired there by the Baron. The action, including a siege of the estate by unruly natives, has about it a strong flavour of Fenimore Cooper. All ends well: Fink marries the Baron's daughter who had once captivated Anton and establishes an outpost of empire in the wild Eastern plains; Anton marries his Principal's daughter and re-enters the commercial fold.

Soll und Haben is an ingenious piece of writing, solidly constructed on dramatic lines in a sequence of easily digestible episodes. The characters range from boldly drawn types to quirkish minor figures modelled after Dickens. Irony and sentiment, realism and glamour—an appropriate sub-title might be 'The Romance of Commerce'—are palatably blended. We are left to infer the date and the identity of the 'capital city' (Breslau) which figures in the story but the vagueness characteristic of the 'Bildungsroman' is otherwise absent. Freytag eschews ideas in favour of action and permits God to make only a brief appearance, on the last page. The fundamental mendacity of the book has been sharply criticized, but German literature is, after all, comparatively deficient in novels which confirm, after the manner of John Buchan's tales, a nation's ideal image of itself.

Freytag, had he kept a restaurant, would have hung out the sign 'gut bürgerliche Küche'—roughly translated, good home cooking. His near-contemporary Wilhelm Raabe (he began writing in the 1850s and is at his best in the short novels produced after 1870) catered instead for the gourmet. This could hardly be inferred from the title of his most characteristic and, to his own mind, best novel. He called it *Stopfkuchen. Eine See- und Mordgeschichte (Stopf-*

kuchen. A Sea and Murder Story, 1891) and built it round a corpulent, voracious hero nicknamed after a particularly stodgy kind of cake; yet this story has the quality, the elusive flavour, and unusual composition which for long delayed a true appreciation of Raabe's work. He likes to involve us in the creation of his stories, to be privy to his subterfuges and we will not, if we know him well, be misled by the sub-title of *Stopfkuchen*. It signals how the story will be written, not what it is about. It is a sea story in so far as it purports to be written at sea; the narrator is a former ship's doctor who has settled in South Africa and scribbles down his memories of a visit to his home town (identifiable as Wolfenbüttel) during a voyage back to the Cape. The voyage is, however, a device for giving depth and amplitude to a narrative compressed into narrow limits of time and space. It takes up little more than a day and revolves around a farm, the Red Redoubt, so called because it shelters behind an earthwork built, overlooking the town, during the Seven Years War. A murderer, whose identity is withheld conventionally enough until the last few pages, figures in the story, but the main function of the murder is to show how the destinies of a seemingly disparate group of human beings can be intertwined. It impinges with varying force on all the characters—the farmer unjustly accused of the crime, his daughter, the rural postman who is the real culprit, the narrator, and his former school-fellow Heinrich Schaumann, the 'Stopfkuchen' of the title. Raabe was not so much a spinner of yarns as a weaver of webs and created in *Stopfkuchen* an intricate structure of intersecting strands, radiating from a human centre—Heinrich Schaumann. He is the most notable of Raabe's many eccentric characters, odd and often unprepossessing creatures by normal standards, born and destined to obscurity, who nevertheless follow their bent and achieve a quality of life which exposes the relative triviality of conventional virtues, aspirations, and graces. Schaumann is a triumphant failure, an enthralling bore. If ever a novel was 'the repository of a voice', it is *Stopfkuchen*; the garrulous hero fills it with his monologues and we and the narrator, like the Wedding-Guest in the *Rime of the Ancient Mariner*, cannot choose but hear. Yet he knows when to hold his tongue: he has long since discovered the murderer's identity, and keeps it to himself until the culprit is safely dead; the most discreet of detectives, he owes it to nobody to tell a pointless truth. The school butt, a hopeless student, a sad disappointment to his parents, he is incompetent and lazy only about inessentials. His boyhood dreams were fixed upon the Red Redoubt, of which he was determined to be master. He realizes them in his own way and in his own time, marries the farmer's daughter, and settles down on his chosen vantage-ground to a life of fruitful idleness.

Raabe's best novels are simple in substance and devious in form. He is not abstruse—he preferred the commonplaces of ordinary people to the profundities of extraordinary minds—but life as he saw it could not be squeezed into the limits of the conventional novel. It could not be chopped up into chapters, so there are none in *Stopf-kuchen*, only occasional shifts in perspective when the narrator lays down his pen. Like Nature, Raabe abhors straight lines and moves tortuously about in time. He does not string together a chain of events. Instead, thoughts and memories flow into each other, drag-ging the events after them; plot is replaced by counterpoint, a com-bination of interlaced story lines. The result is an illusion of life as it is actually lived in our hearts and minds, where past and present mingle and things happen at once rather than in orderly sequence. Raabe was aware that our tolerance of reality is limited—'Give us this day our daily self-deception' was his prayer—but he was in his own fashion a realist. He drew the actualities of his day, the stresses generated by an emergent industrial society, the people and land-scape of his native Brunswick, into his work and moved beyond them, discovering humanity in unlikely places and revealing the common ground on which we rest, divided only by our illusions.

(8)

Robert Louis Stevenson once told Henry James that war ought to be declared on the optic nerve in literature; hearing and feeling, not sight, were what mattered in life and in fiction. He would have taken unkindly to the pictorial prose of the Swiss writer Gottfried Keller, who can imprint an episode or a character on our inward eye with time-defying sharpness. Keller was the son of a Zürich master-carpenter and came to his own craft of literature by way of painting.

He studied art for two years in Munich, gave it up as a bad job, served a laborious apprenticeship to the trade of letters, and combined it in middle life with the post of secretary to the canton of Zürich. He took seven years, from 1848 to 1855, over his first novel, *Der grüne Heinrich* (*Green Henry*) and recast it so drastically in later life that he would have liked all traces of the first version to be obliterated. Towards the end of his life he again tried his hand at a novel, producing after five years of painful labour a period piece, *Martin Salander* (1886), in which his disillusionment with Swiss public life is lightened by no more than a flicker of hope for the future. His natural stature, in painting terms, was that of a water-colourist, adept at recording, in albums of sketches, the changing moods of nature. The literary form at which he excelled was the cycle of stories with a common background or linked by a *leitmotif*. Zürich, its past and its present, the manners and idiosyncrasies of its natives, gave Keller a rich fund of material which he exploited in *Die Leute von Seldwyla* (*The People of Seldwyla*, 1856–74) and his *Züricher Novellen* (1878). His Seldwyla is an imaginary Swiss townlet, whose inhabitants are as genial by nature as their surroundings are idyllic. He surveys their follies and virtues, records their small triumphs and tragedies, and charts their drift into an age of money-grubbing and self-interest. The ten stories which make up the cycle range in scale from blown-up anecdotes with a touch of the fairy tale about them to full-scale 'Novellen'. The tone is predominantly ironic but Keller is capable of true pathos when he has the right material. He wrote nothing better than *Romeo und Julia auf dem Dorfe* (1856), on which Delius based his opera *A Village Romeo and Juliet*. Keller here brings his formidable technique to bear upon an ancient theme—the destruction of a young couple through a family feud. The Capulet and Montague of this Swiss variant are two farmers, whose quarrel over a strip of land ends in their own ruin and the suicide of their only children. Sali and Vrenchen cram a lifetime of happiness into a last blissful and desperate day together. They enact a travesty of the preliminaries to a conventional peasant wedding, dance together for the first and last time in a seedy inn, miscalled the Garden of Paradise, and at nightfall drift downriver together on a hay barge which they have loosed from its moorings.

At daybreak, on a frosty autumn morning, they slip over the side in each other's arms.

If Keller had a fault, it was a perverse disinclination to let well alone. At the end of this factual and unsentimental story, he intrudes himself upon our attention with a bitter comment: when the bodies were washed up, he tells us, the local newspapers reported the event in tones of outraged virtue; it was yet another proof of the evils of a permissive morality. Intolerant only of hypocrisy and uncharitableness, Keller was nevertheless a child of his time. To mirror life was not enough; he had to reflect upon it. He likes to put his characters to ethical tests, doling out appropriate rewards and punishments. He does not spare himself and makes literary capital out of his own blunders, frustrations, and aberrations. An ill-favoured but persistent suitor, he turned his ineffectual search for a fitting soulmate to good account in *Das Sinngedicht* (*The Epigram*), a cycle of marital cautionary tales, and in the best of the *Züricher Novellen, Der Landvogt von Greifensee* (*The Bailiff of Greifensee*). The background is Zürich in the late eighteenth century, colourfully reconstructed, and the hero, Salomon Landolt, is drawn from a well-known 'original' of the period, who embodies the military and manly virtues dear to Keller. The story is a series of interlocking sketches depicting five women who refused the Bailiff's offers of marriage. He assembles his old flames, sits in judgement upon them, and subjects them to an elaborate practical joke, inviting them to select a wife for him, only to announce his intention of remaining a bachelor to the end of his days. *Der Landvogt von Greifensee* was Keller's more or less bland revenge upon womankind; it will be judged arch and smug or a masterpiece of psychological insight according to the sex of the reader.

Uncover the bare bones of *Der grüne Heinrich* and the outline of an uninspiring 'Bildungsroman' seems to be revealed. The hero is Heinrich Lee, nicknamed Green Henry after the colour of the successive suits his mother cut for him from his father's clothing. In early childhood he loses his father, a sturdy and high-principled stonemason and builder, and is brought up by his indulgent mother. Convinced that painting is his vocation, he makes his way from his Swiss village to a German art centre, recognizable as Munich. He gets nowhere with his art studies and neglects his mother, who beggars herself in her effort to support him. Hearing of her plight, he returns home unannounced to find her on her deathbed. Keller first of all kills him off shortly after his mother's death, but in the second version of the novel suspends the sentence; Heinrich abandons painting and settles down in the service of his fellows as a parish administrator. It looks from this as if Keller is 'moralizing the spectacle' of his own life. He draws on his own fatherless youth, his adolescent fumblings with religion and love, his mistaken vocation, his remorse at his treatment of his mother, his dual existence as artist and citizen, and intends these personal experiences to be in some way exemplary. Is Keller, who makes not only Heinrich, but also three of his painter friends abandon art for administration or business, merely saying that the artist, in the broad sense of the word, is fundamentally irresponsible and would be better employed in the public service? If that were so, *Der grüne Heinrich* would be dull reading—but dullness is precisely what Keller was at pains to avoid. His story, he realized, was commonplace; his problem was to tell it in a striking way. He solved it by recourse to a kind of realism hitherto rare in the German novel. *Der grüne Heinrich* is dense with realities, with people and incidents seen in sharp focus instead of through a blur of allegory. The hero has flesh on his bones and blood in his veins and is nourished not on an exclusive diet of ideas but through human contacts. What he has learnt from his experiences is conveyed to us by the way in which he records them, by the clarity, accuracy, and humour with which he tells the story of his childhood, adolescence, and manhood. *Der grüne Heinrich* is stiff with morality, but it is there as a kind of underlay; the true moral of the novel lies in the manner of its telling.

In *Der grüne Heinrich* we see the beginnings of an attempt to depict life as it is rather than life as it ought to be. Compared with Flaubert's *Madame Bovary*, however, which was written about the same time, it has an old-fashioned look; it seems to have been written in a literary backwater. It was only towards the end of the century that Theodor Fontane launched the German novel into the main stream of European realism. Fontane is no Flaubert, no Tol-

:oy; he lacks the disciplined ferocity of the one and the moral
assion of the other. It would never have occurred to him to give
ne of his tales of adultery the motto of *Anna Karenin*: 'Vengeance
; mine, and I shall repay.' Yet he too sees 'other people', society,
; a hard reality instead of a pliant agent in the education of some
Bildungsroman' hero. 'The world is how it is,' says one of his
nany worldly characters; 'things don't turn out the way *we* want
nem, but the way other people want them.' Fontane's world is
'russia during the period of the Second Reich, the world of Berlin,
ne March of Brandenburg, the Baltic coast. The Junkers, the
'russian bureaucracy and officer corps, the *nouveaux riches* who
rospered after the Franco-Prussian war, with a sprinkling of pro-
:ssional men and intellectuals from the lower reaches of the middle
lass are his human material. He strays rarely outside these limits,
nto the past, into Denmark or Hungary, and if he ventures into
vorking-class territory, it is in search of vestiges of instinctive good-
:ss in a hidebound society. Prussian society is the foreground, not
ne background of his novels—a rock-like structure on which indi-
idual passions are bound to founder. Its code of morals and honour,
; sexual conventions, its way of life are the stuff of his best works.
Ie is the first truly social novelist in German literature.

Although Fontane does not set up as a critic of this society, he
as clear likes and dislikes. He is partial to Junkers of the old school,
eats middle-class *arrivistes* with caustic irony and has no time for
ncouth pedants. He does not attack the conventions of Prussian
ociety directly, but exposes their hollowness with the help of
naracters on the social fringe, like the apothecary Gieshübler and
ne maid Roswitha in *Effi Briest*, who embody the ideal of natural
rtue and humanity which lurks in the back of his mind.

His lack of fervour, of any wish to put the world to rights, was
artly inbred; he had always, he said, a well-developed sense of the
nalterable facts of life. It was also the result of his late start as a
ovelist. He was an exact contemporary of George Eliot (he was
orn in 1819) but reached his peak in the age of Henry James,
ardy, and Conrad. He began as a ballad writer, wrote his first novel,
ne historical *Vor dem Sturm*, in his mid-fifties, finished the best-
nown of his stories, *Effi Briest*, when he was seventy-four, and the

last of them, *Der Stechlin*, in 1895, the year of his death. Befor
turning to fiction he had behind him years of experience as a w
correspondent and journalist. He knew England and Scotland we
—he spent four years in London as correspondent for the *Prussia
Gazette*—and explored every inch of his homeland to collect materi
for his *Travels through the March of Brandenburg*. His long a
prenticeship meant that he brought to the novel professional sk
and an abundant store of food for his imagination, one reason wh
he is the least inward-looking of nineteenth-century German writer
Nevertheless, he is an unobtrusive presence among his characte
He sees the human comedy through the eyes of an old man, a
or almost all passion spent, delighting some readers with his urbar
wisdom and irony, exasperating others by a cold-bloodedness whic
is more apparent than real.

Fontane was a realist of the guileful kind. Just as he puts on
show of detachment to make us sympathize more deeply with t
victims of circumstance or human frailty, so he feigns realism
that we may accept more readily his imaginative world. He giv
the illusion of actuality by the use of carefully selected details. H
settings—landscapes, houses, interiors—are economically and accu
ately described. His characters are true to type; they bear the stam
of their place in society, like the central figure of *Der Stechli*
Dubslav von Stechlin, a retired Major, described by Fontane as
typical Brandenburg Junker but of the less strict denominatio
whose family has given its name to the village of which he
squire, the castle in which he lives, and the lake (the 'Stechlin' of t
title) by which it stands. Another is the heroine of *Frau Jenn
Treibel* (1893), on the surface a tale of match-making and matc
breaking, involving the aspiration of a schoolmaster's daughter
marry into the plutocracy, but in fact an essay in portraiture. Fo
tane draws an unflattering but not unsympathetic likeness of
Berlin *bourgeoise*, living in an opulent villa in the lee of her hu
band's pungent chemical works (he manufactures among oth
things Prussian blue), whose hardness of head and acute mon
sense are overlaid by a veneer of sentiment and regard for high
things. The very routine of aristocratic and middle-class life is p
to use by Fontane; the action of his stories is in large measu

geared for dinners, soirées, and picnics, occasions for the conversations which fill his pages and are his chief means of revealing character. Out of such everyday materials, he shapes a world of his own, reducing the confusion of life to carefully calculated patterns. It is in the arrangement and intensification of observed realities that he excels, so constructing novels like *Unwiederbringlich* (*Beyond Recall*) that their end is implied in their beginning and foreshadowed by *leitmotifs* and portentous symbols, like the Chinaman's ghost which haunts, somewhat improbably, the Pomeranian home of the Innstettens in *Effi Briest*.

Love and the lack of it, inside and outside marriage, with the illusions and disillusionment inseparable from it, is Fontane's constant theme. He gives it ironical treatment in *Irrungen Wirrungen* (*Errors, Entanglements*, 1888), the story of a liaison between a seamstress and an officer which ends unsentimentally with the marriage of the one to a rich and vacuous wife, and of the other to an engineering worker and spare-time lay preacher. He explores its sombre side in *Unwiederbringlich* (1891), the most powerful and austere of his novels, set partly in Schleswig-Holstein and partly at the Danish court. The implication of the title is that love, once lost, or thrown away, can never be retrieved. Countess Christine Holkenäs, highly strung, stubborn, virtuous, indeed deeply religious, divorces her adulterous husband, remarries him, under the illusion that she can recapture the happiness of her early married life, and ends by drowning herself in the waters of the Baltic. Clash of temperament is the trouble here. In *Effi Briest* (1895) it lies in the moral code, rigid to the point of inhumanity, of Bismarck's Prussia. In a more permissive age, Fontane would have been short of subjects; as it was, he found a ready source of conflicts in the usages of his time, such as the marriage of convenience. Effi Briest is the victim of such a marriage. The only daughter of a Junker, she is married off at the age of seventeen, by no means unwillingly, to a man twenty years her senior, Baron von Innstetten, upright, ambitious, with most of the usual virtues except love. Isolated, far from home, in the Baron's dismal Pomeranian mansion, a bored and apprehensive child, she has a fleeting affair, conducted with a minimum of passion and a maximum of discomfort, with the local commandant,

Major von Crampas. Nearly seven years later, Innstetten, now risen
to high office in Berlin (Effi herself has become a maid of honour),
discovers her adultery and divorces her, having satisfied honour by
killing Crampas in a duel. After a socially acceptable period of
banishment, her parents let her return home, a sick woman, to
recapture in the brief interval before her death something of the
tranquillity and innocence of her childhood. Fontane gives the last
word to her parents. Sitting in the garden shortly after her death,
they ponder, but not too deeply, its implications. 'Was I in some
way to blame?' asks her mother. 'Was she perhaps just too young?'
Old Briest replies with the phrase he habitually uses when an
awkward question crops up. 'Enough of that, Luise,' he says. 'That
is *too* big a subject.'

Discretion in the discussion of sexual matters was no handicap
to Fontane. A sentence is enough to illuminate the more intimate
side of Effi's life with Innstetten. After a tedious evening spent together, he would 'indulge in a few well-meant but languid caresses,
to which she made no more than a half-hearted response.' He has
no need to labour the details of the adultery; he can skip them the
better to concentrate on the aftermath, the punishment inflicted
by society not only on Effi and Crampas but also on the technically
guiltless Innstetten. Fontane is at his best in the conversation, inser-
ted towards the end of the novel, between Innstetten and Privy
Councillor von Wüllersdorf, his only friend and his second in the
duel with Crampas. Here we see for the first time what a complex,
tormented being Innstetten is, for all his stiffness and pedantry:
here we see the realities of the code, as merciless as it is absurd, by
which he and von Wüllersdorf conduct their lives. Honourable,
eminently successful men, every ambition realized, they are left with
no more than the dubious pleasure of resignation and must make
shift with such small substitutes for happiness as lie within their
reach.

6
The Late Nineteenth Century

(1)

Up to the foundation of the German Empire in 1871, the pace of change in Germany was slow and the structure of society rigid. The prevailing moral code, a compound of Christian ethics with military principles of duty and honour, had hardly been touched by the critical spirit active in theology and philosophy. Literature moved within a narrow orbit of traditional subjects and forms. Change, when it came, was sudden and extreme. The achievement of Great Power status meant that an ethos capable of sustaining the new Empire in peace and war had to be improvised; the industrial revolution was all the more severe in its impact because it was so belated. Writers came up against new problems and areas of experience which confounded old-fashioned notions of art and propriety. As a result, the literary world split up into trends, movements, and schools, for which critical labels such as Naturalism, neo-Romanticism, Impressionism, and Symbolism had to be invented. They had in common a determination to be modern at all costs, although this manifested itself in diverse ways: on the one hand, the attempt to overhaul Zola, Dostoevsky, and Ibsen, and, on the other, the cult of art for art's sake. On the fringe of literature, the criticism of established values coupled with Utopian speculation about the future of mankind, prevalent earlier in the century, took a radical turn towards its end in the work of Friedrich Nietzsche.

Nietzsche should be taken in large doses or not at all; his thought cannot be summarized or illustrated by selective quotation without distortion. He has been the victim of the catchwords he invented or appropriated, like 'the will to power', 'the superman', or 'the death of God' and of our readiness to identify him with the prophet-hero of his major work, *Also sprach Zarathustra* (*Thus spake Zarathustra*, 1883–92). He has never been forgiven for the injunction: 'Thou goest to woman? Do not forget thy whip!', especially by those unaware that it was uttered not by Zarathustra, let alone Nietzsche, but by an old woman intent on remedying the prophet's scant knowledge of the female. The substance of his thought is one thing, its form and direction another. He belongs to literature because he tried to make an art of philosophy and because his chief concern is ethics and the quality of life. He wrote his first book—*Die Geburt der Tragödie aus dem Geiste der Musik* (*The Birth of Tragedy from the Spirit of Music*)—in 1872, when he was still professor of classical philology at the University of Basel. It went far beyond the terms of the title and was among other things a revaluation of the art and temperament of the ancient Greeks; Nietzsche dispelled the associations of noble simplicity and tranquil grandeur which hung around them since the days of Winckelmann and presented them as a people with a unique gift for suffering, who set up tragedy as a defence against despair. *The Birth of Tragedy* was followed by *Unzeitgemäße Betrachtungen* (*Untimely Meditations*), the first of a series of works written, apart from *Untimely Meditations*, in the 1880s, with titles such as *Jenseits von Gut und Böse* (*Beyond Good and Evil*) or *Zur Genealogie der Moral* (*Towards a Genealogy of Morals*), in which Nietzsche combined destructive criticism of the established order with the preaching of his personal gospel. He came of a long line of Lutheran pastors and the mantle of an Old Testament prophet sat easily upon him. He scourges his age, the complacency and Philistinism of Imperial Germany in particular; he foretells disasters to come, railing against the alliance of Church and State in a conspiracy of the weak against the strong; he proclaims the coming of the New Man. As work succeeded work, the scale of his offensive became vaster; the whole of western civilization became his target and when madness finally overtook him he had in mind an 'Umwertung aller Werte', a transvaluation of *all* values. To his critics,

Nietzsche may seem wrong-headed and at best a propounder of unnecessary truths, such as 'One does not hate so long as one despises' or 'There is no feast without cruelty'. His understanding of the operations of the mind is, however, unquestionable. 'It is from our passions that our opinions grow,' he said—a plea that we should see him less as a systematic thinker than as a poet, expressing his moods and fantasies through passionate ideas. He exemplifies his own statement that 'our deficiencies are the eyes through which we see the ideal'. A soft-skinned animal, he offset his defencelessness by puffing himself up and uttering ferocious cries. An inoffensive and bookish person, he had martial dreams and, like W. B. Yeats, chose for his heroes upstanding men. Zarathustra may urge us to 'love peace as a means to new wars' but for Nietzsche, three months as a medical orderly in the Franco-Prussian war (his Swiss citizenship excluded him from combatant service) were more than enough. Like the Kaspar Hauser of Verlaine's poem, he was an untimely man, born either too early or too late, forced to do battle on the ground that was not of his own choosing:

> Quoique sans patrie et sans roi
> Et très brave ne l'étant guère,
> J'ai voulu mourir à la guerre;
> La mort n'a pas voulu de moi.

Nietzsche had no doubt of his literary qualifications; he considered himself the chief among German aphorists, a master of the lapidary style. His ambition was to say in ten sentences what everybody else said, or failed to say in a book, to make his thought immortal by formulating it with Roman concentration and austerity. In practice, he experimented with various media. *The Birth of Tragedy* was a weighty treatise with a coherent argument; *Thus spake Zarathustra* was a gigantic prose poem, rhetorical in style, teeming with similies and metaphors, much of it a pastiche of the Bible. In the later works, he makes use of a form borrowed from the Romantics: the fragment. His natural unit of thought seems to have been the short sequence of reflections, wordy or laconic as the spirit moved him. In a work like *Götzendämmerung oder wie man mit dem Hammer philosophiert* (*The Twilight of the Idols or How to philosophize with the Hammer*, 1889) we can observe his pent-up spirit exploding into aggressive and challenging exaggerations, disguised by a kind of counterfeit logic as arguments. The mood is playful, the purpose iconoclastic; Nietzsche proposes to test the hollowness of contemporary idols—moral, social, psychological, and artistic—with his mental hammer. An introductory run of terse sayings is followed by a series of miniature treatises on such matters as the shortcomings of the Germans or the iniquity of the Sermon on the Mount; these in turn are made up of fragments, haphazard in arrangement and uneven in quality, some pungent, some vapid. Nietzsche's singular way of expressing himself was in line with his hostility to systematic philosophy. Neat systems had been all very well in a rationalist age, when the idea of an orderly universe, governed by discernible laws, patiently submitting to scientific investigation, was still credible; in his own day they were a sign of dishonesty. He pictured the world in *Der Wille zur Macht* (*The Will to Power*) as 'ein Ungeheuer von Kraft, ohne Anfang, ohne Ende', a monstrous force without beginning or end, a sea of energy in perpetual flux, and tried to record its ceaseless motion by a process of high-velocity, random thought.

(2)

Nietzsche constantly lamented his isolation, yet his impact on the generation of writers born in the 1860s and 1870s was powerful. It was felt in the most unlikely quarters—by, for example, Christian Morgenstern and Stefan George, the first a mystic and chief exponent of nonsense poetry in the German language, the second an austere craftsman of forbidding gravity. Morgenstern dedicated his first book of verse to Nietzsche and if his enthusiasm cooled with time he never lost his compassion and respect for him as a spiritual liberator, 'the great antithesis of his age'. Morgenstern himself was sustained throughout his troubled, nomadic existence by his belief in an all-pervading principle of love and by a sense of humour so highly developed as to be an attitude to life: the world was for him an absurd rather than a monstrous force, life a puzzling but absorbing game rather than a grim conflict. There is no lack of precedent for the hazy spirituality of his serious verse, but his *Galgenlieder* (*Gallows*

Songs) have no parallel in German literature, however much they may exploit the peculiarities of the German language and the tortuosities of the German mind. The title is misleading, for there is nothing black about Morgenstern's humour; it derives from a club to which Morgenstern belonged in his early days on the fringe of the Berlin cabaret world—'die Galgenbrüder'. He wrote many of the poems in the first collection, published in 1905, for the entertainment of his friends and much of the later verse when he was busy with the gruelling task of translating Ibsen, Strindberg, and Bjørnson. He inscribed them 'dem Kinde im Manne', quoting Nietzsche to the effect that in every grown-up worthy of the name there is a playful child trying to get out. They are the product of an acute intelligence married to an imagination unburdened by the conventions and distinctions of the adult mind. People, creatures, and things—he is on intimate terms with them all; his birds and beasts, like Emma the Seagull and the Moonsheep, his objects, like the lonely rocking-chair on the deserted terrace, the distraught boots, the amorous bottles, the disembodied knee on its wistful way through the world, share with him and us their anxieties and joys. He plays with language, strips words of their associations, and lets them lead their own life. He telescopes two words in the sentence 'Er ging ganz in Gedanken hin' ('he went along lost in thought') and creates 'Der-Gingganz'; it was simply, he said, taking us for once into his confidence, a German word for ideology. As a rule he resisted interpretation and introduced the *Galgenlieder* with a parody of critical jargon. The poems themselves have an unearthly clarity. Morgenstern, who came of a family of painters, habitually thought in pictures and needed no more than a humdrum object, like the bundle of candles in 'Der Träumer' ('The Dreamer') to set his imagination going:

> Palmström stellt ein Bündel Kerzen
> auf des Nachttischs Marmorplatte
> und verfolgt es beim Zerschmelzen.
>
> Seltsam formt es ein Gebirge
> aus herabgeflossner Lava,
> bildet Zotteln, Zungen, Schnecken.

Schwankend über dem Gerinne
stehn die Dochte mit den Flammen
gleichwie goldene Zypressen.

Auf den weißen Märchenfelsen
schaut des Träumers Auge Scharen
unverzagter Sonnenpilger.

Professor Palmström is one of a pair of amiable characters (the other is Baron von Korf) created by Morgenstern: vague, impractical beings fertile in improbable inventions. Their technological marvels include an auditorium which revolves round a static stage, a philosophical lamp with the property of turning day into darkest night, a musical weighing-machine which plays tunes appropriate to the user; only its inventor, Korf, gets no reaction from it, since he lacks official identity and is thus an imponderable. Time has no terrors for them, for each has a special clock. Korf's has two pairs of hands, one progressive, the other retrogressive, so that time for him is self-suspending; Palmström perfects the Sympathetic Clock which goes back and forth at the owner's whim with a tolerant disregard of temporal principles—a commonplace mechanism, but tender-hearted withal. Morgenstern is their equal in inventiveness; his range covers sheer nonsense, like the plausible gibberish of 'Das große Lalula' or the soundless rhythms of 'Fisches Nachtgesang' ('Fish's Night Song'), satires on officialdom and pedantry, and fantasies, free-ranging but never pointless, for they always have some link with reality. The world in which Morgenstern found himself was a bizarre institution, but no cause for dismay for it was, after all, 'an insubstantial pageant'; human understanding was a poor thing, but what cannot be explained can, after all, be done without. Four lines from the poem 'Täuschung' ('Illusion') give us his philosophy in a nutshell:

Alles ist vielleicht nicht klar,
nichts vielleicht erklärlich
und somit, was ist, wird, war,
schlimmstenfalls entbehrlich.

(3)

Whereas Nietzsche had the role of 'great antithesis of his time' thrust upon him, Stefan George adopted it by choice, and played it out to the end. Born in 1868, he lived on to 1933 and spent his last days in Switzerland, a voluntary exile from the Third Reich. He was a man apart, even in the details of his life-style. An artist-tyrant of priestly demeanour, affecting a kind of poetic uniform, he assembled around him bands of disciples, the 'George Circle', summoned to filter his message through to the common man. The message, encoded in the symbolic language of books like *Der Teppich des Lebens* (*The Tapestry of Life*) and *Der Stern des Bundes* (*The Star of the Covenant*) is of studied vagueness. George denounces the mediocrity and degeneracy of his age; he preaches 'das schöne Leben' the life beautiful, blending Nietzsche's heroic individualism with Hölderlin's Hellenism. One of the last Romantics, like his contemporary W. B. Yeats, he judged life by the standards of art and 'chose for theme traditional sanctity and loveliness.' He believed in the sanctity of language and did much, by example and precept, to furbish up the worn-out diction of German poetry; his poetry validates, however, Morgenstern's observation that too much playing with symbols can make language useless for reality. Even in his last work, *Das Neue Reich*, published in 1928, he is writing poems like 'Der Mensch und der Drud' ('Man and Faun') and 'Das Wort' ('The Word') with the oracular endings: 'Only by magic is life kept awake' and 'No thing exists where the word is wanting.' Try as he might to grapple with the world around him, to move towards simplicity, his habit of mind was not to be changed. He lacked Yeats's ability to discard symbolism when occasion demanded, and capture in unambiguous words the essence of a real situation.

> The best lack all conviction, while the worst
> Are full of passionate intensity—

lines like these, from 'The Second Coming', were beyond him.

If George was an indifferent prophet, he was a linguistic craftsman of the first rank. He was in touch with the leading European poets of his day and assimilated what was most vital in their work. He was one of the founders of *Blätter für die Kunst*, a periodical modelled on the French symbolist *Écrits pour l'art* which appeared intermittently between 1892 and 1919; it sought to give German poetry a new direction, away from the slipshod technique of the Naturalists and the lyrical twittering, to use Turgenev's phrase, of the older generation. His own verse, based on the principles of 'Auswahl, Maß und Klang'—selection, measure, resonance—is disciplined and formal; everything about it, down to the mode of punctuation, the orthography and the type face used, is uncompromisingly poetic. His most memorable poems are petrified moods, or abstract patterns of sounds and images. Sometimes—when, for example, he records his love for the boy poet Maximilian Kronberger—he generates warmth, but he is rarely cordial. 'Masterpieces,' we are told by W. H. Auden, 'should be kept for High Holidays of the Spirit.' Stefan George would not have approved; conscious of his dignity as the great artificer, he made it his business never to relax. He is a distant figure compared with Rainer Maria Rilke, who began writing in the same period; whereas Rilke reaches out into the twentieth century, George's idea of beauty and faith in Art stamp him clearly as a man of the 1890s.

(4)

Towards the end of the century the German theatre was seized by a fit of innovation. Up to the 1880s, dramatists were content to follow well-trodden paths; then Büchner was rediscovered, Ibsen and Strindberg were transplanted to Germany, ancient dramatic conventions were discarded, forbidden areas were opened up in defiance of orthodox taste and the censor. Within a generation, the Expressionists were setting the pace in the European theatre and cinema. Three writers born in the 1860s, Gerhart Hauptmann, Arthur Schnitzler, and Frank Wedekind, all played a part in the business of modernization.

Hauptmann's enormous output—he wrote over forty plays, a score of prose works, and much epic and lyrical verse—resembles a museum of style; he began as a realist, veered off into symbolism, reverted to realism and ended in the 1940s with a visionary epic, *Der große Traum* (*The Great Dream*) and a cycle of plays on Greek themes, *The Atridae*. His first play, *Vor Sonnenaufgang* (*Before Sunrise*), was produced in 1889 by the 'Freie Bühne', a Naturalist theatre club in Berlin, modelled on the Parisian 'théâtre libre', which had opened in the same year with Ibsen's *Ghosts*. This 'social drama', as Hauptmann called it, deals with a Silesian peasant family grown rich and dislodged from its milieu by the discovery of coal under its land. It ends with the suicide of Helene Krause, one of the daughters, when her lover, the high-principled socialist economist Dr. Alfred Loth, realizes that the family is tainted with hereditary alcoholism. *Vor Sonnenaugang*, however significant for the development of the German theatre, now seems an uneasy compromise between old and new dramatic fashions. The trappings were novel: Hauptmann plays upon current ideas about the conditioning of character by heredity and environment; he reconstructs the Krause milieu in elaborate detail; he uses dialect and aims at life-like speech. The modish externals conceal, however, an antiquated tragedy of common life, designed to move the spectator to compassion and tears. German Naturalist drama never matched the extreme demands of some of its theorists and remained soft-centred. It was not long before Wedekind in Munich was deriding its tameness and Schnitzler in Vienna was practising a much subtler kind of realism.

In his novels, stories, and plays, Schnitzler observed Viennese society at the end of the century with a scientific yet compassionate eye. He recorded its more sinister as well as its mellower aspects, dealing, for example, with the problem of anti-Semitism in his novel *Der Weg ins Freie* (*The Way to Open Country*, 1908) and in *Professor Bernhardi* (1912). As an analyst of psychological disturbance, an explorer of the borderland between illusion and reality, he is a notable but not exceptional figure in modern Austrian literature; it is as an anatomist of love that he excels. He trained as a doctor in Vienna when accepted views of personality and behaviour were being challenged, and not only by Sigmund Freud: we find Nietzsche, for example, acknowledging that the degree and quality of our sexuality penetrates even the upper reaches of our minds. It was also a time of powerful sexual taboos, hard to imagine nowadays when freedom is limitless on stage and screen. In England, Shaw remarked, dramatists were expected to deal almost exclusively with cases of sexual attraction, 'yet forbidden to exhibit the incidents of that attraction or even discuss its nature'. In Germany, a hint of incest and the off-stage birth of a still-born child in *Vor Sonnenaufgang* were enough to outrage prim susceptibilities. In *Anatol* and *Reigen* (*The Round Dance*) Schnitzler trod this treacherous ground with a delicate foot.

He began *Anatol*, his first work, in London in 1888 and finished it in 1891. It is a sequence of seven dramatic episodes, each involving a different woman, with Anatol's friend Max feeding and interrupting the hero's self-revealing monologues. Anatol is a Viennese bachelor, idle in all but love and the hunt for some fixed point in the flux of life. He combines a genius for self-deception with a habit of self-analysis; he cannot, so Max tells him, enjoy the present because he bears too heavy a burden of unassimilated past. For ever railing at the faithlessness of women, he nevertheless nurses the illusion that he can demand of them what he himself cannot offer—unconditional surrender; he is chronically jealous, yet would not be otherwise for he is a hypochondriac of love. *Anatol* is a case-history of what Robert Burton in the *Anatomy of Melancholy* called 'love-melancholy'; *Reigen* (1900) develops the theme of sexual egotism, exposing both its consistency and the variety of subterfuges it uses to get its way. It is a cycle of ten interlocking dialogues between ten characters from different strata of Viennese life who hand each other on like partners in a round dance: the Prostitute who pairs off with the Soldier in the first episode reappears in the last as the partner of the Count. The figures of the dance—anticipation, consummation, satiation— never change and the dancers, as they circle around us, are scarcely distinguishable one from another. They would be tedious company were it not that their common inability to give themselves away in love is matched by their readiness to give themselves away in speech. When he was writing *Anatol*, Schnitzler took as his model the French dialogue of Ludovic Halévy, Offenbach's librettist; he refined it, gave it a Viennese gloss and by the time he wrote *Reigen* had perfected a type of casual, laconic, yet infinitely revealing conversation rare in the German theatre.

Unlike Hauptmann and Schnitzler, Wedekind was a professional entertainer. He gives off an unrefined odour of greasepaint and saw-dust. He toured Europe with a circus in his youth, sang his own songs to the guitar in Munich cabaret, and became an actor with his own repertory company. A crude performer, apt to fluff his lines, he was nevertheless able, so Bertolt Brecht tells us, to fill the stage with his personality; his appearance—the lugubrious owlish eyes set in rigid features—and his rasping voice were unforgettable. A natural clown, he longed to be taken seriously by the bourgeois spectators he set out to shock. He attacked their hypocrisy, preferring the hectic vitality of crooks and whores to the pallid virtue of the respectable, and paraded before them what he called 'the fifth estate', a class beyond the social pale, unburdened by moral and social scruples. His message is neither original nor coherent; his view of man as the prisoner of his own institutions, born and dying in slavery, sewn up in a strait-jacket at birth, nailed up in a coffin at death, goes back at least as far as Rousseau's *Émile*. He was neither the first or the last writer to agitate for a sexual revolution and champion instinctual morality. More remarkable than his message is his use of the theatre, which anticipates many features of modern drama. He mixed a number of styles, realistic and grotesque, sentimental and satirical, farcical and tragic, directing them all to the same end: a powerful impact on the audience.

His first notable play had the ironic title *Frühlings Erwachen* (*Spring's Awakening*, 1891). Its theme is the impact of puberty on a group of children brought up ignorant of the mysteries of sex—tender blossoms blasted by conventional morality and parental prudery. The fifteen-year-old Wendla Bergmann dies after an abortion arranged by her mother; her tombstone, inscribed 'Blessed are the pure in heart', records her death from 'anaemia'. Moritz Stiefel, ridden by anxiety and guilt, kills himself. His friend Melchior Gabor, respons-ible for Wendla's pregnancy, survives, for this 'Kindertragödie' has a more or less happy ending. In a macabre final scene Melchior's thoughts of suicide are symbolized by his conversation beside Wendla's grave with the ghost of Moritz Stiefel. His trust in life is restored by a mysterious figure, 'der vermummte Herr', whose mask does little to conceal Wedekind's own features. *Frühlings Erwachen* is a sympathetic account of adolescence, seen as a moment of crucial change in the cycle of life when instinct and morality violently collide. Asked by Melchior for his views on morality, 'der vermummte Herr' defines it as the real product of two imaginary quantities, 'Sollen und Wollen', moral obligation and desire. Like Wedekind he questions the origins and validity of the prevailing 'system of pieties'; he has no illusions about its reality and strength.

Raw sexuality is the theme of *Lulu*, a tragedy in two parts, *Erdgeist* (*Earth Spirit*) and *Die Büchse der Pandora* (*Pandora's Box*) which Wedekind finished in 1902. Lulu is the embodiment of an elemental force, innocent yet terrible, like the Earth Spirit in Goethe's *Faust*. Greek mythology provided a symbol for her destructive potential: the story of Pandora, whose precious box was imprudently opened by her husband Epimetheus, whereupon a host of evils and disasters was loosed upon humanity. Wedekind appears in the prologue as an animal-tamer, enticing us into his menagerie by showing us his prize specimen, the snake Lulu, a wild and beautiful creature much more alluring and vital than the domesticated exhibits on view in the contemporary theatre. He shows us Lulu in action in Berlin and Paris, leaving behind her a train of human wreckage, including three husbands and a miscellany of lovers, and finishes her off in London, a prostitute, with Jack the Ripper as her last client. The destroyer is herself destroyed by the society which perverted and abused her innocence. Wedekind used in this tragedy a technique of violent distortion which was to have many imitators. The Expressionist playwrights who followed him shared his confused moral passion but lacked his theatrical cunning; their plays are at best a pale reflection of the nightmare world of *Lulu*.

One of Wedekind's favourite roles was the confidence trickster hero of his tragi-comedy *Der Marquis von Keith*. He finished the play in 1900, in prison on a charge of *lèse majesté*, the result of writing for *Simplicissimus* an indiscreet poem on the Kaiser. Keith, adopted son of a nobleman, natural son of a sharp-witted intellectual and a gipsy, is finally bested by the Munich tycoons whom he had thought to defraud. Ordered by one of them, Konsul Casimir, to get out of Munich within twenty-four hours, he toys with the idea of suicide but thinks better of it; he lays his pistol aside, accepts the scape money offered him, and goes on his unrepentant way. His friend Graf Trautenau, on the other hand, opts out of life. A wealthy aristocrat and fanatical moralist, he aspires to be a useful member of society; he is cured of his illusions, comes to his senses—and retreats to a lunatic asylum. Although Keith is by temperament an enemy of society, he embodies its predatory and unstable nature. Money is for him the root of all good and property the source of all ideas. 'Sin,' he says, 'is no more than a mythological term for bad business.' He is much given to aphoristic sayings and sums up his view of life as a choice of evils in the comment: 'Der Mensch wird abgerichtet oder er wird hingerichtet.' Wedekind died in 1918, at the end of the Great War, by which time the notion that we must submit, or be executed, had become more than a dramatist's fancy.

7
The Twentieth Century

(1)

FUTURE historians of literature are likely to have trouble in findin
a term to describe the temper of the twentieth century. A label suc
as 'The Age of Anxiety' which suggests itself for the first half of th
period would sit awkwardly on the last couple of decades; they coul
better be called, at least in Germany 'The Age of Distrust'. See
from another point of view, the twentieth century has been an age o
exploration and technical experiment. Phases and fashions, many o
them originating in German-speaking territory, have followed eac
other with dizzy rapidity. With the disappearance of generall
accepted beliefs, values, and norms of taste, the traditional literar
genres have fallen apart. In drama, the void left by the death o
tragedy has been filled with strange hybrids—black comedy, th
theatre of the absurd, epic theatre, and documentary theatre—
cultivated by writers like Brecht and Weiss, Frisch, Dürrenmatt, an
Hochwälder. In narrative literature, conventions of plot and char
acterization have been discarded and such has been the pace o
change that 'the new novel' is already outmoded. The competition o
more powerful media has induced in many poets a mood of despon
dency; some, modelling their habits on the hermit crab, have with
drawn into their shells to engage in enigmatic monologues, emerg
ing from time to time to converse with their intimates or writ
poems about the difficulty of writing poetry. Popular verse has bee
left to the song-writer. The best-known German poem of the centur

was written, not by some Rilke-like luminary, but by the obscure Hans Leip; 'Lile Marleen,' one of his love-songs, written in 1915 and popularized in the thirties through a series of broadcasts entitled 'Poetry set to Music', resounded over the battlefields of the Second World War and can still be heard echoing throughout the world.

Writers in the German language have had to contend both with the unstable literary climate of our time and with the pressure of circumstances peculiar to themselves. German literature has been profoundly affected by the sequence of events set going by the First World War—the collapse of the Hohenzollern and Habsburg Empires, the calamitous interlude of National Socialism, the suffering and devastation which it caused, and the political fragmentation of Germany after 1945. The impact of the First World War on German culture was violent, but not wholly destructive; the war coincided with what has come to be known as the modern movement in the arts, which continued in Germany during the brief life of the Weimar Republic and was arrested by the National Socialist campaign against 'degenerate art' in the mid-thirties. The impact of the Second World War was much more severe. When it ended, writers who had been dispersed by exile, captivity, 'inner emigration', or conscription were slow to rally their forces. Moreover, many of them were left in a state equivalent to surgical shock; they suffered from a paralysis of confidence in their craft, in its ability to express the terrible realities which obsessed them. Even Paul Celan, for all his assured technique and will to communicate, acknowledged that his poetry was too slight a vessel to hold the enormity of his experience. His grief at the suffering of his fellow Jews overflows the limits of 'Todesfuge' (Fugue of Death), his best-known poem, a set of variations on a grim theme—'Der Tod ist ein Meister aus Deutschland'—arranged in a complex structure of images and sounds. If 'Todesfuge' has a flaw, it is that over-ingenuity of form by which we can, perhaps, measure Celan's suspicion of his medium. Where plain speech might have served him better and moved us more, he uses highly condensed metaphors, combining motifs drawn from the Book of Lamentations and the dance of death in elaborate counterpoint.

Such after-effects of the war were to be expected. Less predictable was the result of the division of Germany into two states with ideologies so different that the very foundation of literature, language, has been affected. The time has come when East German literature since 1945 has to be treated as a separate entity. Nevertheless, the best writers on both sides of the frontier have a common characteristic: a sharp eye for fraudulence and inhumanity, a distrust of the efforts made in the West to cosset them, and in the East to coerce them, into conformity.

(2)

Between 1910 and 1925, German literature went through one of its phases of Storm and Stress. It was announced by the appearance in Berlin of weekly reviews whose titles, *Der Sturm*, *Der Demokrat*, and *Die Aktion*, promised an explosion of dynamic energy, and it acquired more by accident than design the name of Expressionism. Up to 1914, the term was applied to the kind of painting in which the appearance of things is violently distorted by emotional stress and mental agitation; it was then used to identify the work of a group of writers bound less by clear principles and a common style than by the vague but powerful feelings which possessed them. German Expressionism was a stream fed by both foreign and native sources. Traces of French and Italian *avant-garde* movements, of older writers like Whitman and Strindberg can be found in it, but in its extreme form it had an inwardness and intensity which owed nothing to influence from abroad. There is among the early Expressionists a strong sense of 'the world-engine creaking and cracking', as Auden put it in *The Age of Anxiety*. Strengthened by a sense of personal corruption, it fills the poetry of Georg Trakl, with its splintered syntax and lurid colour-symbolism, its visions of desolation and glimpses of a spiritual order beyond the chaos of the world. It is communicated by the dislocated imagery we find in 'Weltende' (World's End), a poem by Jakob van Hoddis (the pen-name of Hans Davidsohn) which appeared in the first number of *Der Demokrat*:

> Dem Bürger fliegt vom spitzen Kopf der Hut,
> In allen Lüften hallt es wie Geschrei.
> Dachdecker stürzen ab und gehn entzwei,
> und an den Küsten—liest man—steigt die Flut.

Der Sturm ist da, die wilden Meere hupfen
an Land, um dicke Dämme zu zerdrücken.
Die meisten Menschen haben einen Schnupfen.
Die Eisenbahnen fallen von den Brücken.

Such presentiments of doom were all too accurate. Many German
and Austrian artists and writers were victims of the First World
War, Trakl among them: he took his own life while serving with the
Austrian medical corps in Galicia, after the battle commemorated in
one of his finest poems, 'Grodek'. As for Davidsohn, after years
spent in mental hospitals he was murdered by the Nazis in 1942.

During and after the war the key changed and a new, ecstatic note
was struck in Expressionist poetry and drama; angry protests
against soul-destroying materialism, high-pitched appeals to
humanity combined with Messianic proclamations of the New Man
and Utopian visions. 'Sturz und Schrei', 'Erweckung des Herzens',
'Aufruf und Empörung', 'Liebe den Menschen'—collapse and cry,
the heart's awakening, exhortation and outrage, love of mankind—
these were the movements into which Kurt Pinthus divided *Menschheitsdämmerung* (*The Dawn*, or *Twilight of Humanity*), the
'symphony' of Expressionist poetry which he published in 1919.

Menschheitsdämmerung was probably the Expressionist anthology
which so depressed Franz Kafka; these poets, he said, stretch out a
hand to humanity, but all that humanity sees is a clenched fist.
Although Kafka belonged in point of age to the Expressionist
generation, he stood outside the movement, repelled by its stridency.
'Such a small book and so much noise'—his comment on a book of
poems by Albert Ehrenstein, entitled *Der Mensch schreit* (*Man
cries aloud*) touches on the weakness of much Expressionist writing,
especially for the theatre. Even in the best plays of the period, like
Georg Kaiser's *Von Morgens bis Mitternachts* (1912) or his trilogy
Gas (1918–20), the message is drowned by a hubbub of words. As a
result, Expressionist drama made its impact less through its substance
than through the methods of production and design it inspired and
through its influence on early film technique.

(3)

There is nothing strident about Kafka. He set great store by tranquillity and kept the pitch of his writing correspondingly low, redressing the obscurity of his meaning by the clarity of his prose. He is less of a problem to disinterested readers than to those under an obligation to interpret him. The critic will be doing well if he manages to utter even half-truths about him. Although he has been credited with creating a new kind of fiction to express the predicament of modern man, he will seem to some readers as much concerned with the timeless realities of the human condition as with twentieth-century anxieties and doubts. As for his fiction, its novelty is a matter of the way Kafka puts ancient forms to strange uses. In novels like *Der Prozeß* (*The Trial*) and *Das Schloß* (*The Castle*) and in many of his shorter pieces, he uses the myth, the parable, and the fable, which were invented long ago to communicate truth and read a meaning into life, to symbolize the elusiveness of the one and the senselessness of the other. Not that his influence on modern literature, on the theatre as well as the novel, is in question; he has had many imitators, especially among writers with delusions of significance who have sought to reproduce the quality of his vision. He has, moreover, added a word to our vocabulary—Kafkaesque, with its associations of being lost in a maze of corridors leading nowhere, of impotence in face of unintelligible forces, of beating our heads against invisible walls.

Kafka was born in Prague, into the Jewish community which formed an enclave within a larger enclave, the German-speaking minority in the Bohemian capital. His orbit was narrow. He once looked down on the old city from a window and said to a friend: 'There is my school, opposite it is my university, and a bit to the left is my office. My whole life is enclosed within that little circle.' Prague meant to him what Dublin meant to Joyce, but unlike Joyce he was never seriously tempted to cut loose from his native city— that 'little mother with sharp claws who never lets you go'. His father, whose transfigured shape looms large in Kafka's dream-world, ran a fancy-goods store in Prague and Kafka himself earned his living as a lawyer with the Workers Accident Insurance Institution for the Kingdom of Bohemia. He contracted tuberculosis, was pensioned off in 1922, and died two years later in an Austrian sanatorium. A timely end, for it spared him the fate of his three sisters, who were deported and killed after the Nazi occupation of Czechoslovakia.

Kafka spoke of literature as an expedition in search of truth and his own exploration of this uncharted territory is recorded in many of his writings. In *Die Prüfung* (*The Test* or *The Examination*) he appears as an unemployed servant, envious of those who, no more pushing or zealous than himself, are summoned, whereas he endlessly awaits the call. Interrogated over a drink at an inn by a fellow servant, he finds that he cannot understand the questions, let alone answer them, and disconsolately rises to take his leave. 'Don't go,' says his interrogator. 'That was only a test. The candidate who does not answer the questions has passed the examination.' If a novel like *Das Schloß* (pub. 1926) seems to raise unanswerable questions, we can take comfort from this parable about the importance of being ignorant. Few symbols in modern literature have had stranger interpretations than Kafka's Castle. It dominates the life of the land-surveyor K., just as it dominates the life of the village at which he arrives, in the belief or delusion that he has been appointed to work there. Kafka never finished his account of K's persistent, frustrated efforts to legitimize his position and make direct contact with the authorities in the Castle, but he hinted at a provisional solution: on his deathbed, K. was to get word from the Castle that he was permitted, not by right but by an act of grace, to live and work in the village. To ask what the Castle means is like asking who is the Godot who never turns up in Samuel Beckett's play. In *Waiting for Godot*, the meaning is in the waiting; all that is certain about the Castle is that it is a seat of power, a subject on which Kafka himself was an authority. Elias Canetti says of him: 'Of all writers, Kafka was the greatest expert on power. He experienced it and fashioned it in all its aspects.' The observation occurs in a perceptive study entitled *Der andere Prozeß* (*The Other Trial*), centred upon an episode in Kafka's prolonged and abortive engagement to Felice Bauer—the 'court' in the Hotel Askanischer Hof in Berlin to which Kafka was summoned by the Bauer family in the summer of 1914;

it reappears, like a reflection in a distorting mirror, in the inaccessible court which tries the bank official Joseph K. in *Der Prozeß*. *Der Prozeß* (pub. 1925) is an example of Kafka's talent for transmuting intimate humiliations into symbols of general significance. It is the most self-centred of his stories, the tale of a trial in which he is at once defendant, judge, and jury, ending up as his own executioner, an investigation, it may be, of his own consciousness and the limitations of his art. Nevertheless, we can perceive at least an aspect of ourselves in Joseph K. He is neither as exceptional as his creator nor as inscrutable as his judges and what he undergoes is a public, not a secret trial.

Stubborn enough in defence of the freedom and loneliness he needed for his writing, Kafka was in other respects a vulnerable man. He felt an affinity with small defenceless creatures, wrote about mice as well as men, and made an insect of repellent aspect the hero of his best-known Novelle, *Die Verwandlung* (*The Transformation*, 1916). 'When Gregor Samsa awoke one morning from uneasy dreams,' the story begins, 'he found himself in his bed changed into an enormous beetle.' This extraordinary occurrence is treated as a matter of fact and its consequences, both for Gregor and his family, are recounted in the unembellished, basic German which Kafka habitually used. *Die Verwandlung* is a tragic, but not a dismal fable; it is enlivened by Kafka's peculiar brand of desperate irony. After Gregor's death and the hasty disposal of his unsightly remains, his parents and sister, housebound for months, take a tram ride into the country and give themselves up, the nightmare over, to dreams of a rosy future.

(4)

Kafka was one of a group of writers born in Austria or Bohemia in the 1870s and 1880s who would figure prominently in a full-scale history of German literature. The most conspicuous member of his generation, which included Felix Braun, Hermann Broch, Robert Musil, and Hugo von Hofmannsthal, is Rainer Maria Rilke. Rilke's impact on European poetry was considerable; so too was his ability to make disciples of his readers. He has been called, and by one of his more critical admirers, the greatest German poet since Hölderlin.

Although the cult of which he was once the object has now gone the way of other substitute religions, he is unlikely to be forgotten by his fellow poets. He belongs to the same literary species, now extinct, as Stefan George, but is a more authentic specimen of the poet-seer. For all his apparent fragility and helplessness, he pursued his poetic mission with ruthless determination. It is hard to tell if his poetry is a reflection of his life or his life a reflection of his poetry. His Narcissism, or as he put it, his egoism, was positively heroic; despite many changes of style and standpoint, he kept to one subject—himself and his inner life. In his massive correspondence no less than in his poetry he gives us the illusion of wishing to communicate with others, and is in fact using the letter—one thinks in particular of the *Briefe an einen jungen Dichter* (*Letters to a Young Poet*) and the *Briefe an eine junge Frau* (*Letters to a Young Woman*)—as an elegant means of self-clarification. His need of loneliness was as great as Kafka's—he described it as a kind of work or vocation— but he wanted to be loved as well as lonely; he pursued, through an endless series of relationships, an ideal of 'besitzlose Liebe,' demanding of others an utterly undemanding love. He once wrote to a friend: 'The successes and insights which coincide happily in a poem or other work of art are no proof of ability to master the problems of daily life.' He nevertheless acted out with remarkable consistency that belief in art as ideal existence which is stated, in extreme form, in the third of his *Sonette an Orpheus*:

> Gesang, wie du ihn lehrst, ist nicht Begier,
> Nicht Werbung um ein endlich noch Erreichtes;
> Gesang ist Dasein. Für den Gott ein Leichtes.

Some of the difficulties we meet in Rilke proceed from his habit of making capital out of his own creative processes. He cloaks the occupational disorders of the poetic life in elaborate symbols and can turn the experience of being stumped for words into a disaster of cosmic proportions. In 'Der Dichter', however, he sums up the poet's lot in plain words:

> Ich habe keine Geliebte, kein Haus,
> keine Stelle, auf der ich lebe.
> Alle Dinge, an die ich mich gebe,
> werden reich und geben mich aus.

Rilke was born in Prague, left it when he was twenty, rarely revisited it and was at pains to erase from his life-style the marks of his humdrum origins—his father was an employee of the Turnau –Kralup–Prague Railway Company. In so far as he had a base during his wandering life it was Paris. He first visited it in order to write a monograph on Rodin and had an uneasy but poetically fruitful association with the sculptor, whom he served briefly as a part-time secretary. Rilke settled in Switzerland in 1919 and died there in 1926. Between 1902 and 1910 he produced, in addition to various prose works, two collections of verse, *Das Buch der Bilder* (*The Book of Images*) and *Neue Gedichte*, and a cycle of quasi-religious poems entitled *Das Stundenbuch* (*The Book of Hours*), consisting of 'The Book of Monastic Life', 'The Book of Pilgrimage', and 'The Book of Poverty and Death'. The matter of the *Stundenbuch* is a complex of ideas which germinated in Rilke's mind early in life, took shape during his visits to Russia, and were fully developed in his later poetry. He takes the traditional concepts of God, death, and immortality and bends them to fit his personal creed, of which the first article was: there is no God but Art and the Poet is His Prophet. *Das Buch der Bilder* is a miscellany, made up chiefly of mellifluous mood-poetry, with a sprinkling of poems in the more objective, sculptural style of the *Neue Gedichte*. The two volumes of the *Neue Gedichte* contain many of Rilke's best-loved poems, among them 'Der Panther', 'Das Karussel', and 'Die Flamingos'. Apart from odd lapses into the grandiloquent or the exquisite, he mantains an extraordinary level of craftmanship. He had learnt from Rodin, to whom the second volume is dedicated, to 'work from Nature'; he schooled himself in the art of patient and penetrating observation and applied it, in the *Neue Gedichte*, as rigorously to works of art and to Biblical and mythological themes as to nature, content for once to subordinate himself to the matter of his poetry.

The castle of Duino, high above the Adriatic not far from Trieste, has had some strange tenants; at the end of the Second World War, for example, it was used by the British Eighth Army as a corps head-quarters. Rilke had the run of it during a critical phase of his life and it was here that he began the *Duineser Elegien*, a cycle of ten poems which took him ten years to complete. The *Duino Elegies* were his most ambitious undertaking, a 'Reading of Life' on the grand scale, a distillation into highly condensed figurative language of his terrors and hopes, doubts and affirmations. They are impalpable stuff, all the more difficult to grasp because Rilke operates from so exalted a standpoint; he stands on a height, at the extreme limit of human consciousness, from which all conventional distinctions, including the distinction between life and death, dwindle into insignificance. What could not be contained in the *Elegies* overflowed into the *Sonnets to Orpheus*, a set of fifty-five variations on Rilke's habitual themes, composed within the space of a few days. The elegiac note persists, but the *Sonnets* as a whole are a celebration of life, with all its deprivations, and a song in praise of song:

> Nicht sind die Leiden erkannt,
> nicht ist die Liebe gelernt,
> und was im Tod uns entfernt,
>
> ist nicht entschleiert.
> Einzig das Lied überm Land
> heiligt und feiert.

(5)

In one of his *Letters to a Young Poet*, Rilke warns against the indiscriminate use of irony. It is a useful servant and a dangerous master. If it looks like getting out of hand, there is only one remedy against it: 'Seek out the depths of things; they are beyond the reach of irony.' Similar advice is offered to the young hero of Thomas Mann's novel *Der Zauberberg*; since, however, *The Magic Mountain* is a parody of the 'Bildungsroman' and since the advice is given by an untrustworthy mentor, an ironical intention can be suspected. For Thomas Mann, irony was a habitual attitude of mind; he applied it to the depths as well as to the surface of things and above all to his own work. He expressed wonder, in an autobiographical sketch, at the honours heaped upon him by society; he was after all only a writer, one of a species not only useless but positively inimical to the State, an unruly, disreputable charlatan who deserved and expected to be treated with silent contempt. Instead, he found himself rewarded with riches and esteem. This was doubtless to his advantage, but it was not as it should be; it must be an encouragement to vice and a thorn in the flesh of virtue. Perverse sentiments, it may be thought, coming from the weightiest German novelist of the twentieth century, but they are none the less heartfelt. Mann wrote much about 'Art', about its morally suspect sources and the perils of the artistic life. He had an ideal of sound, and therefore great, art and regarded Goethe and Schiller as exemplary because they fought their way to some kind of balance between intellect and instinct, yet he never quite rid himself of the suspicion that there was something fraudulent about the whole business.

Mann's pervasive irony was among other things a way of reconciling the conflicting sides of his personality. His friend Hermann Hesse, writing to congratulate him on his eighteenth birthday distinguished between his estimable and his endearing aspects. He was a respectable figure because of his bourgeois qualities of self-discipline, diligence, and patience (his 'Hanseatic' virtues Hesse called them, alluding to Mann's forbears, who were well-regarded Lübeck grain merchants). What made him lovable was the unbourgeois, irresponsible part of him, his irony, his delight in play, his zest for impossible literary adventures undertaken in the full knowledge that they were impossible. Mann brought off the difficult feat of being at once ponderous and capricious. His major writings are heavy with thought and literary reminiscence, and even in his short stories, Novellen, and essays, he made a point of giving intellectual value for money. As to subjects, he flits from one to another, his nimbleness increasing rather than diminishing with age. The centrepiece of his work is *Joseph und seine Brüder*, (*Joseph and his Brothers*, 1933–43) a cycle of four novels in which Mann reconstructed the world of ancient Israel and Egypt, applying a modern intelligence to the Old Testament story. On either side of *Joseph und seine Brüder* lie the Goethe novel *Lotte in Weimar* (1939) and *Der Zauberberg*, (1924) in which a Davos tuberculosis sanatorium serves Hans Castorp as a school of life. The common factor in this group of novels is their moral intention: they are stages in Mann's attempt to resolve the dissonances he detected in himself and, by extension, in modern civilization. They were preceded and followed by two studies in dissolution. *Buddenbrooks* (1901), his first novel, is the history of four generations of a Lübeck merchant family whose vitality is sapped by progressive spiritualization until art takes over from life and the line dies out; *Doktor Faustus* is an allegory of the decline and fall of National Socialist Germany. His choice of themes for his later novels, written when he was in his seventies, was erratic to a degree. *Der Erwählte* (*The Elect of God*, 1951) is a stylistic escapade, a travesty of a medieval legend: Hartmann von Aue's *Gregorius*. *Die Betrogene* (*The Deceived Woman*, 1953) is a morbid parable about the ambiguity of Nature's intentions towards humanity; sparing us no clinical detail, Mann tells the story of a widow at the change of life whose apparently miraculous rejuvenation is induced by cancer of the pelvic organs, and leaves us to judge if the growth is malignant or benign. His last novel, the unfinished *Bekenntnisse des Hochstaplers Felix Krull* (*Confessions of Felix Krull, Confidence Trickster*, 1954) is in a totally different key; it is Mann's most entertaining tale, a blithe allegory of the artistic life, a piece of self-persiflage, and a parody of his own style.

Mann published a fragment of *Felix Krull* as early as 1911. It was one of a series of stories written in his twenties and thirties, dealing with the problem of the artist in a variety of modes ranging from the comic to the tragic, among them his delicately drawn 'portrait of the artist as a young man', *Tonio Kröger*. Thanks to Luchino Visconti's film and Benjamin Britten's opera, *Der Tod in Venedig* (*Death in Venice*, 1911) is likely to become the best known of them. Deservedly so, for the composition is masterly in the true sense of the word. Mann is in complete control of his material; every superfluous detail has been whittled away; the style, the structure, the setting, and the central character are all of a piece; every episode portends the death of Gustave Aschenbach in cholera-stricken Venice. Aschenbach is an ageing writer with all the classical virtues, austere, well balanced and a master of his toilsome craft—he is used in the schools as a model of style. He is 'der würdig gewordene Kunstler', an artist who has battled his way to dignity. His laboriously constructed moral defences collapse under the impact of Eros, come to life in the shape of Tadzio, a fourteen-year-old Polish boy. He dies of the plague of love, tempting prey for those uncontrollable forces whose pleasure it is to trample on human dignity and reason.

Mann left Germany in 1933 and spent the remainder of his life in Switzerland and the United States. It was in California that he wrote *Doktor Faustus* (1947), the 'tragical history' of the German composer Adrian Leverkühn, told by his friend Serenus Zeitblom, a retired schoolmaster. Mann uses Zeitblom's pedantic, slow-moving, and humane mind as a lens through which to view the career, the descent into madness, and the death of Leverkühn, the most complex of his artist figures, for he is both cut off from normal humanity and a mirror of the corrupt society in which he lives. In *Doktor Faustus* Mann set himself the formidable task of representing symbolically the spiritual disintegration of Germany between the wars and his novel is inevitably congested with ideas; he worked into it many of his obsessions—the Faustian nature of the German soul, the notion of music as the quintessential and peculiarly German art, the correlation of art and disease, genius and madness, the precarious foundations on which our civilization rests. It is, in a sense that Mann may or may not have intended, his most ironical work: over-elaborate, oblique rather than direct in its treatment of reality, hovering between the profound and the abstruse, it hints at the very qualities of mind which hastened the catastrophe it records.

Whereas Mann's stock has fallen in recent years, Hermann Hesse's has risen, especially among young people. Intolerant of direction, yet searching for guidance, they have turned to him as a wise and congenial guru, enveloped in cloudy spirituality, who understands their problems and offers them an ideal of personal integrity. Hesse came of evangelical stock (his father and grandfather served as missionaries in India) and described his own temperament as fundamentally Christian. His mind was nurtured on German Pietism, the wisdom of the Vedanta and the Tao, and the psychology of Jung, and in so far as his work had a purpose it was to find and proclaim the true way. A Swabian by birth, he settled in Switzerland and from his retreat in Montagnola sent out into the world a stream of novels, short stories, and poems carrying his message that our self, our individuality, is the sole reality of our life. Like a Germanic Peter Pan, he refused to grow up. In early novels and stories such as *Unterm Rad* (*Beneath the Wheel*, 1906) and *Kinderseele* (*A Child's Soul*, 1917), he recaptured the joy and torment of boyhood and adolescence and even in old age he kept his belief in 'delight and liberty, the simple creed of childhood'. He was not blind to the cruelty of Nature, but preferred to depict her in her gentler moods, as Frau Eva, a mother figure from whom we have our being and to whose all-embracing arms we must finally return. He distrusted what he called the over-organized machinery of the modern State and had a horror of violence; he never ceased to wonder at the amount of organization, method, and rational thought which went into the senseless business of war. He was the natural ally of vagabonds and misfits, dreamers and drop-outs, like Harry Haller in *Der Steppenwolf*, a lone wolf of a man isolated from the herd in the hell of his inner being. *Der Steppenwolf* (*The Wolf of the Steppes*, 1927) recorded a personal crisis, the crisis of Hesse's fiftieth year—one reason why it caused, he tells us, more misunderstanding than any other of his novels. Young readers could make little of the problems and fantasies of middle age, while readers old enough to identify themselves with Haller grasped only half the author's meaning and missed the faith behind the despair. Although the main character is so finely drawn, *Der Steppenwolf* is an ungainly story. The self-portrait is blown up into a symbolic figure and Haller's sickness of the soul becomes the neurosis of his generation, the sickness of the times themselves. Like its hero, the novel has 'one dimension too many'.

Hesse worked from memory and imagination and kept within a narrow range of types and problems, returning to them again and again at different stages of his experience. It was, he said, the tension he felt within him between 'Leben' and 'Geist', life and spirit, which drove him to continuous self-analysis and self-revelation. He embodied these incompatible principles in a succession of characters and made the relation between them the theme of *Narziß und Goldmund* (1930). The novel takes us back into the world of Novalis's *Heinrich von Ofterdingen*—the romantic Middle Ages—and begins and ends in the monastery of Mariabronn. At the heart of the story is the love of Narziß, novice and later abbot of the monastery, the personification of intellect, for his pupil Goldmund, a creature of instinct and impulse, incapable of abstract thought, and destined to be a maker of images. While Narziß keeps within the confines of the monastery, bound by a regimen of order, service, and rigorous thought, Goldmund explores the world, tastes its joys and sorrows, and learns the craft of wood sculpture from Meister Niklaus, finding in great art that fusion of instinct and pure spirit which is unattainable in reality. Finally, all passion spent, he returns to the monastery to die, attended by his friend. *Narziß und Goldmund* has been highly praised for its flawless structure. It is, if anything, too immaculate, too high-minded. Narziß's love for Goldmund, Goldmund's erotic adventures with a series of buxom wenches, glowing Jewesses, and high-born ladies, are handled with positively embarrassing delicacy. To the cruder kind of literary palate, the novel, with its pre-digested philosophy and its transparent symbolism, will seem bland to the point of insipidity.

It was natural for a writer of Hesse's quality to try his hand at a full-scale 'Bildungsroman' of the allegorical sort. He wrote *Das Glasperlenspiel (The Bead Game)*, his last major work, during the decade 1932–42 as he watched the submersion of the humane values he prized under a tide of violence. The novel is set, at a distant point in time, in a mythical region—Castalia—which has a strong resemblance to the educational province in Goethe's *Wilhelm Meister*. The 'bead game' is played by the members of a lay order, supported by the state, devoted to the preservation of tradition and the education of a cultural élite; a synthesis of the arts and sciences, based mainly on music and mathematics, it is a highly abstract form of training in method and intellectual discipline. In so far as the novel has a plot, it is woven around Joseph Knecht (his name means 'servant'), an orphan who works his way through the hierarchy until he reaches the topmost rank, Magister Ludi, Master of the Game. Disenchanted by the sterility, the remoteness from life of the order, he gives up his office to educate the son of his friend Designori, a former member of the order turned man of action, but he is drowned swimming in a lake with his pupil before he can begin this practical mission. *Das Glasperlenspiel* will be found subtly ambiguous or vague, topical or a museum-piece, according to the reader's disposition. It is based on a familiar formula, the antithesis of life and mind and appears to lead by an excessively tortuous route to the conclusion that the human spirit cannot thrive cut off from reality. To judge the novel by its message would, however, be unfair; the message is less important than the reflections which envelop it. *Das Glasperlenspiel* is the distillation of Hesse's thought about the nature of the human personality and the forces, including education, which can make or mar it.

(6)

By the end of the Second World War, the fabric of literature, together with much else in Germany and Austria, was in ruins. The writers who came back from exile and captivity, or from the obscurity of 'inner emigration' faced a formidable task of demolition and reconstruction. The year of defeat and collapse, 1945, became known as 'der Nullpunkt', zero, the point from which a fresh start had to be made. A clean sweep had to be made of the fraudulent and inhumane ideology of National Socialism; the liberal values it had all but destroyed had to be revived and society rebuilt on new foundations; some way had to be found of re-entering the mainstream of European literature from which Germany had long been cut off and on a more practical level the apparatus of literary life, dislocated by the war, had to be restored. The launching, in 1946, of the periodical, *Der Ruf (The Call)* was a step in this direction. Published in Munich, and sub-titled 'Independent Journal of the Young Generation' it was the continuation of a periodical of the same name started towards the end of the war in the United States with the general aim of re-educating prisoners of war. It was the mouthpiece of a generation for whom the exposure of past illusions and the appraisal of present realities were a prelude to the rehabilitation of Germany on liberal socialist lines. The editors, Alfred Andersch and Hans Werner Richter, fell foul of the American military government of Bavaria and an attempt to replace *Der Ruf* by a satirical journal, *Der Skorpion*, broke down. The outcome was the formation of Gruppe 47, possibly on the model of the earlier Gruppe 25, a coterie which had included Brecht, Musil, and Kaiser. Group 47 was an informal association of writers which met regularly up to 1967 and is now, after a period of inactivity, showing signs of renewed life; it had a fluid membership, including East German writers, held together by a critical attitude to established authority and a determination that the past should not be discreetly buried in the pages of history books. The founders of Group 47 are now middle-aged but vestiges of the original spirit remain: a quarter of a century after the collapse of the Hitler regime, attempts are still being made to conjure up the 'Zeitgeist' which engendered it and to chronicle the war to which it led, with its aftermath of social and spiritual confusion. Two writers associated with the Group, Günter Grass and Heinrich Böll, will serve to show what diverse methods have been applied to the common task of enlightenment and social criticism.

Grass's first novel, *Die Blechtrommel* (*The Tin Drum*) had a *succès de scandale* when it appeared in 1959. It touched many a sensitive nerve; its bawdiness, although no more than incidental and innocent enough by present standards, offended squeamish readers; it was decried as tedious and obscure—'a Teutonic nightmare'—and praised for its exuberant invention and rich texture. *Die Blechtrommel* is a novel of the three-ply sort: a satire on the most disastrous phase of German political and intellectual history, a parable about Grass's own estrangement from society, and an evocation of the milieu (ever present in his stories) in which he spent his youth— Danzig in the thirties and forties. Grass, needing a hero who would weave together the public and private strands of his novel and who would also give us a worm's-eye view of the German world, settled for a dwarf. Oskar Matzerath recounts his life, from his birth in Danzig to his thirtieth year, from his bed in a Düsseldorf mental home, where he is confined on a dubious charge of murder. He is a voluntary dwarf; at the age of three, when he was given his first tin drum he took steps to arrest his growth, thereby opting out of the adult world with its associated ideologies and taboos. Lilliputian of body, he has an outsize mind; he is a Simplicissimus in reverse, born fully mature, with a mighty voice, capable of shattering brittle illusions, and a talent for drumming up the past and tapping out the rhythms of the present. Small though he is, he dwarfs most of the outsiders in modern literature; he sees the world from a strange angle, with merciless and indiscriminate objectivity. He has been written off, unfairly, as totally inhuman. In fact, he puts on a few inches in the course of his life and dreads the moment when he will be discharged into the world from the security of his asylum and have to assume full stature.

Die Blechtrommel was followed by *Katz und Maus* (*Cat and Mouse*, 1961), a fragment hewn from Grass's later novel *Hundejahre* (*Dog Years*, 1963). They form a trilogy of sorts, covering the period from the mid-twenties to the mid-fifties. They have the same West Prussian background; characters overflow from one story to another —Walter Matern, barely perceptible in *Die Blechtrommel*, takes on monstrous proportions in *Hundejahre* as an agent of Nemesis, scouring post-war Germany accompanied by his hell-hound Pluto, once Hitler's companion in the Wolfsschanze and the Führerbunker; each story moves by a different route over much the same ground to the same destination; each ends on a muted note of loneliness.

Grass, a sculptor, graphic artist, poet, and playwright before he took to the novel, commands many techniques and a vast fund of verbal energy. He is capable of simplicity—*Katz und Maus* is an orthodox Novelle—but prefers complexity. The critics, he complains, confuse novels with automobiles and require them to run as smoothly as a Mercedes, whereas he wants to give us an uncomfortable ride. Blending realism with allegory, grotesque images with precisely observed details, he can convey, sometimes all too effectively, the muddle and tedium of life as he sees it. His stories are given substance by his great power of recall, and piquancy by his talent for linguistic parody and pastiche: ingredients from all stages in the evolution of the German novel, from Grimmelshausen to Thomas Mann, with a dash of Swift and Sterne thrown in, can be detected in his prose.

In his latest novels, Grass, now in his mid-forties, puts away his Sturm und Drang and faces up to a new generation of Germans— unburdened by guilt, impetuous and impatient, intolerant above all of explanations. In *Örtlich betäubt* (*Local Anaesthetic*, 1969) a forty-year-old Berlin schoolmaster surveys, from the prison of a dentist's chair, his dismal record of compromise, his failure to communicate with the pupils he tries to anaesthetize against the pain of existence; a liberal Marxist, addicted to the pain-killing drug of Stoic conformity, he seems to them an ineffective sham, 'a paper tiger'. *Aus dem Tagebuch einer Schnecke* (*From the Diary of a Snail*, 1972) tries to bridge the generation gap with the help of a political parable, told by Grass to his children on his return from an election tour in the Social Democratic interest. In his new-found role of pedagogue, he gives them a lesson in scepticism, teaching them distrust of ideological fanatics and of those 'final solutions' exemplified, terribly, by the extermination of the Danzig Jews. As a symbol of his doctrine of progress, his unheroic revisionism, Grass chooses the snail— lymphatic, slow-moving, credited in mythology with healing powers —and commends its virtues to his German pupils. Whereas there were flashes of the old ferocity in *Örtlich betäubt*, *Aus dem Tagebuch einer Schnecke* begins with the words: 'Dear Children' and continues in a tone of fatherly benevolence. Yesterday's *enfant terrible* has turned model parent and time has once more shown its ability to take care of most angry young men.

Post-war German prose writers have, like Grass, found it hard to clarify their experience; it is as if they had been pressurized into complexity by the need to shed oppressive memories of the past, the attempt to reproduce the confusion of the present and the urge to keep abreast of literary trends. Straightforward narrative, of the kind thrown up by the First World War, is rare; we find instead linguistic virtuosity, tortuous construction, and opaque symbolism. Until recently, Heinrich Böll stood out among his West German contemporaries by virtue of his relative simplicity. He is the eighth German writer to receive the Nobel prize for literature (the others included Thomas Mann and Herman Hesse) and the award, made in 1972, had a mixed reception in Germany, where Böll had a reputation for triviality, substantiated in the view of hostile critics by his immense popularity. Up to the 1960s, he practised an unpretentious kind of realism, less concerned with ambitious technical experiments than with his mission as a Christian moralist. Since the appearance in 1961 of *Billard um halbzehn* (*Billiards at half-past nine*) there have been signs of conformity to the fashion for ostentatious originality. His *Gruppenbild mit Dame* (*Group Photograph with Lady*, 1971), is a novel of ample proportions; using an elaborate technique of *collage*, he constructs a panorama of the German scene from the 1920s to the present day and assembles a representative array of characters who bear witness to the life of the central figure—one of the obscure heroines of our time who crop up frequently in his work.

Böll began as an exponent of 'Trümmerliteratur', the literature of debris, the wreckage left behind by the tide of war. The suffering of soldiers and civilians alike on the Eastern front, the plight of war-widows, orphans, and maladjusted ex-servicemen, the corruption and callousness bred by war, the senselessness of military life—especially if you have the misfortune to be on the wrong side—these are the themes of his early stories and novels. During the period of Germany's economic miracle, Böll turned a critical eye on the complacent materialism and rat-race ethos of the affluent society, saved from an excessive display of moral outrage by his strong sense of humour; it found an outlet in the satirical stories he wrote in the 1950s, ironic commentaries on the specious efficiency and cultural absurdities of the technocratic age.

As a moralist, Böll prefers the less obtrusive virtues; as a novelist, he keeps clear of spectacular action and abnormal personalities, content to give distinction to the unremarkable and lend a voice to the inarticulate; he is a deft craftsman, able to create a convincing illusion of everyday experience, in which memory colours our perception of the present and routines and rituals serve to slow up the flux of time. He keeps in general to familiar ground, using the Rhineland and his native city Cologne for most of his characters and settings. One of his most revealing books is not, however, about Germany at all; it is his *Irisches Tagebuch* (*Irish Diary*, 1957), a perceptive, warmhearted, and flattering tribute to his spiritual home. Ireland is for Böll 'a piece of Catholic Europe outside the pale of the Roman Empire' where the churches are hideous but well used, and where God is either loved or hated, but never ignored, where poverty is real, but of no consequence, and where inefficiency is a virtue. His silence about the less attractive features of the Irish psyche is characteristic, for he has some difficulty in accommodating evil within his scheme of things. He operates from a secure base—his firm, but by no means uncritical Catholic faith.

The first novel in which Böll clearly showed his hand was *Und sagte kein einziges Wort* (1953). On one level it is a piece of 'Trümmerliteratur', the record of a marriage disrupted by the war; on another it is a 'Legende', an episode in the life of a latter-day saint. Käte Bogner is one of the meek who have somehow failed to inherit the earth, a model of mute suffering in the face of tribulation —the title of the novel comes from a Negro spiritual she hears on the radio:

> They nailed him to the cross, nailed him to the cross
> And he never spoke a mumbling word.

Her troubles are two: poverty and love. With her three surviving children, she leads a drab existence in a war-scarred city, bound by the sacrament of marriage to a shiftless husband. Fred Bogner, one of nature's deserters, has abandoned her in characteristically half-hearted fashion; they still meet at week-ends, making joyless love in ruined houses and squalid hotels. He is a man benumbed by war, apathetic, and obsessed by death. His trouble is a general paralysis of feeling, cured, if only temporarily, by the unspectacular miracle with which the novel ends. Once an army telephonist, transmitting death-dealing messages from one staff officer to another, he has the same job in civilian life, manning the exchange in a diocesan headquarters from which the Church conducts its cautious manoeuvres between God and Mammon. Whereas his religious faith is vestigial (he can only pray when he is drunk), Käte's is the reality which governs her life. Like her uncouth parish priest, who is rated 'Gamma minus with a tendency to Delta' by the clerical establishment, Käte Bogner is an authentic Christian—one of a rare species living in obscurity on the fringe of religious orthodoxy.

The best and the worst of Böll are to be found in *Und sagte kein einziges Wort*. His sentimentality and lugubrious religiosity can be disconcerting: it is during a bout of morning sickness that the pregnant Käte has her clearest vision of God, who could, since all time is at His disposal, have chosen a better moment to reveal Himself. But such lapses are the price we pay for the clarity and the ability to extract significance from commonplace lives which make Böll the most readable annalist of his time.

(7)

Günter Grass celebrated the five-hundredth anniversary of Albrecht Dürer's birth by writing a set of variations on the theme of the engraving 'Melancholia I'. Entitled *Vom Stillstand im Fortschritt* (*On standing still in the midst of progress*, 1971) they were a defence of melancholy (associated in Grass's mind with a sceptical view of progress) against those Utopian political systems which seek to suppress it; he had in mind both capitalist states like America, where happiness is a branch of big business and Communist states like the German Democratic Republic, where it is decreed by the central committee of the party. Since the foundation of the Republic in 1949, East Germany has been the scene of a vast experiment in social engineering, in which literature is an important agent; its function is to create a positive ethos and esprit de corps, to reflect the social and economic progress of the state, to teach the principles of socialist morality, and to stiffen morale. To judge by the massive encyclopedia of East German literature which appeared in 1971 we now have to reckon with a substantial body of writing, with distinctive characteristics and a history of its own, which merits less superficial treatment than can be given it here.

The pioneers of East German literature were writers like Arnold Zweig, Anna Seghers, Johannes Becher, and Bertolt Brecht who returned after the war from exile in Palestine, Mexico, the Soviet Union, or the United States to play their part in the construction of the first German socialist state. They belonged to a generation born between 1880 and 1900 and were more at home with the tribulations of the past than with the problems of the present; there is, for example, a marked difference in quality between Anna Seghers's powerful story *Das siebte Kreuz* (*The Seventh Cross*, 1942), which deals with the escape of seven prisoners from a concentration camp, and later novels like *Die Entscheidung* (*The Decision*, 1959), which deals with divided Germany. Their successors, working chiefly through the medium of the novel and the short story, operate as observers on various sectors of the social front; they write of the stresses and strains produced by the new order in village, farm, and university, of frictions within the family, of the clash between individual freedom and social responsibility, and can be judged more fairly as practitioners of applied rather than pure literature. Novelists like Erwin Strittmatter and Hermann Kant have a markedly traditional quality; orthodox in technique and conservative in outlook, they have the air of survivors from the Age of Enlightment, when art was the servant of morality and when literary eccentricity was bad form. In the German Democratic Republic, literary trends reflect the alternation of freeze and thaw in cultural policy, but the effect of political pressure on East German writers can be overestimated; while they may find it hard to reconcile socialist realism with official demands for exemplary characters and happy endings, their main difficulties are the same as those of their West German contemporaries. Young poets like Günter Kunert lament the impotence of the lyric compared with the crude power of the mass media and feel they are launching their verse into an unresponsive void; prose writers grapple with the problem that has faced German novelists since the eighteenth century—the intractable material offered to them by German society.

Except for Johannes Bobrowski and Bertolt Brecht, who is in a class of his own and resists any kind of regional classification, East German writers have found it hard to produce work of more than localized interest and documentary value. Bobrowski, who died in 1965, grew up in what used to be known as East Prussia, in a region with a mixed population of Germans, Jews, Lithuanians, Poles, and Russians colonized in the Middle Ages by the Teutonic Knights; he served with the Wehrmacht on the Eastern front and was for eight years a prisoner of war in Russia. His verse makes an unusual impression of amplitude, partly because of his broad vision, partly because he sets much of it in the boundless land he calls Sarmatia— the name given by Roman historians and geographers to the territory between the Vistula and the Volga, stretching south to the Caucasus, a vast area inhabited in ancient times by nomadic tribes. His writings are scanty—they include a few short stories, the two books of poetry *Sarmatische Zeit* (*Sarmatian Time*, 1961) and *Schattenland Ströme* (*Shadowland Streams*, 1962), and the novel *Levins Mühle* (*Levin's Mill*, 1964), set in a West Prussian village in the 1870s—but of consistently high quality; his style is terse, his images precise, his perspective deep. His general theme was the relationship between Germany and the European East; his purpose was to tell his country-men something about their Eastern neighbours and to make visible the wrongs inflicted upon them in the distant and immediate past. Bobrowski pursued his task of enlightment and conciliation un-obtrusively, kept clear of remorseful breast-beating or political sermonizing, and concentrates on writing well and truthfully. He created a world without frontiers, peopled by men and women who turn out, once we have got used to their unfamiliar accents, to be our own kith and kin.

Bobrowski had no more than a lukewarm admiration for the plays of Bertolt Brecht, whereas he rated his poetry highly. This view of the outstanding German playwright of the first half of the century is not as eccentric as it seems; it is gaining ground and it may well be that Brecht will be remembered as a poet long after all but his best plays have become period pieces and his dramatic theories are lost to view in histories of criticism. He was a specialist in the art of com-munication. He had no taste for the interior monologue or the inner landscape and his general line in his earlier poetry is the argument or public address. His late poems have a more private quality, but his social concern is undiminished and if he speaks of intimate matters it is because he considers them in some way exemplary; in the guise of a benign, sagacious elder, he gives the human family the benefit of his experience. As a poet and as a playwright his chief care was to write effectively. He set little store by originality and in one of his anecdotes commended a Chinese philosopher who wrote a book of a hundred thousand words, nine-tenths of it made up of quotations. 'We can no longer write books like that,' he commented, 'we aren't intelligent enough.' Acquisitive by nature, he purloined any scraps of literary material that came his way; he was fond of adapting plays by other dramatists (among them Shakespeare, Farquhar, and John Gay) and employed an assortment of stylistic models—the Bible, sixteenth-century ballads and Berlin cabaret songs, Rudyard Kipling and François Villon, Chinese and Japanese poetry. He used the full compass of the German language and a variety of styles, including, in his early verse, an anti-style of calculated awkwardness. For his later poems he devised a variable metre based on natural speech-rhythms and a type of diction prosaic enough to make his meaning clear and poetic enough to be memorable. He could fashion poetry from prosaic material, even from his own dramatic doctrine, and summed up the purpose of his work in an address to Danish worker actors on the art of observation: their task and his was to observe and demonstrate the nature of man, the better to lead them and teach them the great art of living together.

It is impossible to typecast Brecht; descriptions of him as a Communist or as 'a rebellious son of the bourgeois West' are over simplifications. He turned to Communism in the 1920s, after service in the First World War, because it suited his mind and his sensibility it offered him a cure for the injustice and suffering which outraged his reason and his compassion, a key to the understanding of histori cal change, and an acceptable kind of discipline. There was a strain of destructive scepticism in him against which Marxism was a useful but only partially effective antidote. As Martin Esslin said of him in *The Theatre of the Absurd*, 'he never succeeded in suppressing the pessimistic anarchist within himself and it is from the tension between his two selves that his greatest poetic and dramatic power springs'. If he took readily to Marxism it was because he was pre disposed to materialism and his habit of mind was naturally dialec tical. He was a born activist and even if he had never read Marx' *Theses on Feuerbach* he would doubtless have believed that the purpose of art, as of philosophy, is to change the world and not merely interpret it. This was the principle on which he based his view of the function of the theatre in our time.

Brecht left Germany when Hitler came to power and returned in 1949 to East Berlin. At the Theater am Schiffbauerdamm he founded, together with his wife Helene Weigel, the Berliner Ensemble and created a school of production which had a powerful influence on world theatre. The intention was to turn the theatre into a tribunal, with the spectators cast as dispassionate observers collaborating actively in the proceedings instead of wallowing in emotion. But Brecht never forgot that the main business of the theatre is entertainment and often discarded his theories in favour of the ancient principle that you must stir the spectator's heart before you can improve his mind. The social satire of *Die Dreigroschenoper*

The Threepenny Opera, 1928), the most likely candidate for
urvival among Brecht's early works, would make little impact
vithout the ballads and the music by Kurt Weill which support
hem. As for the great plays which Brecht wrote during his years of
xile—*Mutter Courage und ihre Kinder* (*Mother Courage and her
Children*, 1939), *Leben des Galilei* (*The Life of Galileo*, 1938), and
Der Kaukasische Kreidekreis (*The Caucasian Chalk Circle*, 1945)—
nly the most hardboiled spectator could sit through them unmoved.

None of Brecht's writings gives a clearer insight into his mind
han the anecdotes entitled *Geschichten vom Herrn Keuner* (*Tales
f Herr Keuner*, 1930–56). His Herr Keuner is a self-portrait, dis-
orted here and there by caricature, exhibiting all his intellectual
oibles and prejudices. Whereas he detests cats because they are so
nisanthropic, he loves elephants, and hints, by means of a catalogue
f elephantine virtues, at the way he would like us to regard him.
The elephant combines cunning with strength; it leaves a broad
rail wherever it goes; it has a thick skin and a tender disposition; it
as adjustable ears—it hears only what suits it; it is inedible; it does
omething for art—it supplies ivory. By way of a testament, Brecht
eft us his poem 'An die Nachgeborenen' ('To Posterity'). It is an
ccount of how he spent the years granted him on earth, in a dark
ge when to talk about trees was almost a crime since it involved a
lence about so much brutality, when those who sought to prepare
ne ground for kindliness could not themselves afford to be kind. It
nds with a plea for charitable understanding on the part of those
vho, in the distant future, may be lucky enough to live in a more
umane age:

> Ihr aber, wenn es soweit sein wird
> Daß der Mensch dem Menschen ein Helfer ist
> Gedenkt unsrer
> Mit Nachsicht.

Translations

---

p. 27   Man, become essential; for when the world is at an end, accident will fall away. Essence will endure for ever.

p. 27   I know that without me God cannot live for an instant; if I come to nothing, he must expire for need of me.

CHAPTER 3

p. 31   I am your creator, am wisdom and goodness, a God of order and your salvation; these are my qualities! Love me with your whole heart and share in my grace.

p. 32   My being is stirred, O God, by a gentle tremor of Thy omnipresence. My heart and my frame tremble less violently. I feel, I feel it, that even where I weep, there too art Thou, O God.

p. 48   How happy I am in Rome, remembering the time back in the north when grey days enveloped me and the gloomy, lowering sky weighed upon my head, when a colourless and shapeless world lay around me and I withdrew listlessly into contemplation, exploring the dark by-ways of my dissatisfied mind.

p. 49   The outside world offers either too much or too little. Only at home is everything within bounds.

p. 50   The man who aims at great things must take himself in hand; the master needs limitation to bring out the best in him, and only law can give us freedom.

p. 51   When I was a little boy, I used to walk at midnight, not exactly willingly, past the churchyard to the parson's house, my father's; star upon star, they all shone so beautifully at midnight. When I was further afield in the expanse of life and had to go to my lover—had to, for she drew me irresistibly—the stars and the northern lights battled above me and coming and going I breathed in happiness: at midnight. Until at last the light of the full moon penetrated my darkness so brilliantly and distinctly that my thoughts too wove themselves round the past and the future, willingly, meaningfully and swiftly: at midnight.

p. 52   Your oddities will stick to you of their own accord; what you ought to be cultivating are your good qualities.

p. 52   See with what strange contortions people rack themselves. Nobody wants to become something; we all want to be something from the start.

p. 52   Great passions are incurable illnesses. It is the remedy for them that makes them so dangerous.

p. 53   He who feels no love must learn to flatter.

p. 53   There is nothing more terrible than ignorance in action.

p. 57   Talent develops in solitude, character is formed in the press of life.

p. 57   If you want to discover the exact nature of propriety, then all you have to do is to ask a lady of noble mind. Men strive for freedom, women for good morals.

p. 59   All theory, my friend, is grey, the tree of life is green and gold.

p. 59   If I ever say to a moment in time: You are beautiful, stay for ever, then you can put me in chains, then let there be an end of me.

p. 60   To that moment in time I would be prepared to say: You are beautiful, stay for ever ... In anticipation of such matchless happiness, I now enjoy the supreme moment.

p. 60   So you got through; well, you made it, anyhow. Anyone else would have broken his neck.

p. 61   What is this I feel? I am borne aloft by gentle clouds, my heavy armour as light as a summer dress. Upwards, upwards—the earth drops away—the pain is short-lived and the joy eternal.

p. 61   Cardinal, I have done what I had to do. It is now your turn.

p. 67   This business was too grave in its beginning for it to end in nothing. So let things take their course.

p. 68   Be steadfast in the face of dire suffering, give succour to the innocent in distress, keep eternal faith when you have sworn an oath, be true to friend and foe, keep your manly pride before the thrones of kings at the cost, if necessary, of life and property, let merit have its due, let there be an end to all enemies of truth.

p. 69   Whither have you vanished, world of beauty? Come again, sweet age when Nature was in flower!

p. 71   Meanwhile it often seems to me better to sleep than to be without companions as we are. I cannot bear this time of waiting and do not know what to do or say in the meantime, and what use are poets in a time of dearth?

p. 71   Alas, where am I to get, when it is winter, the flowers, the sunshine and shadow, of the earth? The walls stand speechless and cold, the weathercocks clatter in the wind.

p. 72   The God is near and hard to grasp. But danger and deliverance from danger are to be found growing upon the same ground.

p. 72   The seafarer returns happily to the quiet river from the distant islands where he has harvested; that is how I would come home if I had earned as much wealth as sorrow. Dear river banks, once upon a time you brought me up; can you ease the pain of love? Woods of my childhood, can you promise me peace once more when I return?

CHAPTER 4

p. 86   No sooner has the noisy merriment of man been silenced than the earth, through the rustling of all its trees, begins to call up in us things of which the heart is barely conscious, old times, tender grief, and faint tremors of dread flicker through my breast like summer lightning.

p. 86   When God wishes to show special favour to a man he sends him out into the wide world, so as to show him his wonders in mountain and wood and river and field.

p. 86   I am content to let God guide me; He who sustains the streamlets, larks, woods and fields and earth and sky has also arranged things to *my* best advantage.

CHAPTER 5

p. 92   You are like a flower, so pleasing and beautiful and pure; I look at you, and melancholy steals into my heart.

p. 92   I do not know what it means that I am so sad; an old-time fairy tale keeps running through my head.

p. 92   A young man loves a girl who has chosen another; this other young man loves somebody else and has married her. Out of pique, the girl marries the first fellow she can lay her hands on; the young man is in a sorry plight. An old story, but it never grows stale; and anyone who happens to relive it will have a broken heart.

p. 93   Frenchmen and Russians own the land; the British own the sea. But we in the airy realm of dreams hold undisputed sway.

Here we are supreme, here we are unpartitioned; the other nations have developed on solid earth.

p. 94   All I ask for, Lord, is health and extra pay! O let me live happily on with my wife for many a day in the same old way!

p. 94   O God, cut short my suffering, so that they can soon bury me; after all, you know that I have no talent for martyrdom.

p. 95   Sleep is good, death is better—the best thing, of course, would be never to have been born.

p. 104   Man's point of origin, the end he comes to, the forces he hides within his heart, the forces his heart conceals from him, that is the content of our solemn play.

p. 105   I feel too weak to struggle on. Give me the victory, spare me the battle.

p. 106   In the early morning, when the cocks crow, I have to stand at the range and light the fire. The glow of the flames is lovely, the sparks fly; I do no more than stare, sunk in grief. Suddenly, faithless boy, it comes back to me that I dreamt of you last night. Then tear after tear pours from my eyes; and so the day comes—if only it would go away again!

p. 108   I think of this and that, I am filled with longing, I do not know for what: it is half pleasure, half mourning; tell me, o my heart, what memories you are weaving in the twilight of the golden green branches!—old times of which I do not care to speak!

p. 108   The misty world is still at rest, the wood and the meadows are still dreaming: soon, when the veil falls, you will see the blue sky clearly revealed and the subdued world, its autumnal energies released, suffused with warm gold.

p. 109   Send what you will, oh Lord, happy or sorrowful things! I am satisfied that both should flow from your hands. But do not overburden me with joys or with sorrows, for somewhere in the middle lies sweet contentment.

p. 119   A little fir tree is growing, who knows where, in the wood, a rose bush, in who can tell which garden. They have already been picked out—ponder this, my soul—to take root and grow upon your grave. Two little black horses are grazing in the meadow, they prance friskily back to the village. They will go at a walk with your corpse, perhaps, perhaps even before the horseshoes loosen that I can see gleaming on their hooves.

CHAPTER 6

p. 135   Although lacking a fatherland and a king and somewhat lacking in courage, I wanted to die in war; death would have nothing to do with me.

p. 137   Palmström puts a bundle of candles on the marble top of his bedside table and watches them melting away. Mysteriously they turn into a mountain range of down-flowing lava, form tufts, tongues, scrolls. Flickering over the molten wax the wicks stand flame-topped, like golden cypresses. On the white cliffs of fairyland the dreamer sees bands of intrepid pilgrims of the sun.

p. 138   Everything may not be clear, nothing perhaps explainable, and so what is, will be and was, is at the worst dispensable.

CHAPTER 7

p. 148   The bourgeois's hat flies off his bullet head, everywhere the air echoes with a screaming sound. Tiles crash down from roofs and split in pieces, and—so one reads—the tide is rising on the coasts.

    The storm is upon us, the wild seas leap ashore to smash thick dams. Most people have a cold. Trains and their tracks drop off the bridges.

p. 153   Song, as you teach it, is not desire, not the courting of something after all attained; song is existence. An easy matter for the god.

p. 153   I have no lover, no home, no place in which I live. All things on which I expend myself become rich and expend me.

p. 155   We do not know the meaning of suffering, we have not learnt to love, and what carries us away in death remains a mystery. Song alone upon earth hallows and celebrates.

p. 171   But you, when a time comes, in which men will be helpers of men, remember us with charity.

Bibliography

THE following list is a selection of books, mainly in English, on German literature. Many of the outstanding works written from the seventeenth to the twentieth century are collected in *Klassische deutsche Dichtung*, F. Martini and W. Müller-Seidel (eds.), 22 vols. (Herder, Freiburg-Basel-Wien, 1961–9). English translations of German works are listed in *The Penguin Companion to Literature 2, European Literature*, Anthony Thorlby (ed.) (Penguin Books, London, 1969), and in *Cassell's Encyclopaedia of World Literature* (Cassell, London, 1973). For background material, see *Germany. A Companion to German Studies*, Malcolm Pasley (ed.) (Methuen, London, 1972), and W. Walker Chambers and John R. Wilkie, *A Short History of the German Language* (Methuen, London, 1970).

HISTORIES OF GERMAN LITERATURE

August Closs (ed.), *Introductions to German Literature*, 4 vols. (Cresset Press, London, 1967–70). H. B. Garland, *A Concise Survey of German Literature* (Macmillan, London, 1971). W. Kohlschmidt, *Geschichte der deutschen Literatur* (Reclam, Stuttgart, 1965). F. Martini, *Deutsche Literaturgeschichte von den Anfängen bis zur Gegenwart*, 16th edn. (Kröner, Stuttgart, 1972). J. M. Ritchie (ed.), *Periods in German Literature* (Wolff, London, 1966). J. G. Robertson, *A History of German Literature*, 6th edn. by Dorothy Reich (Blackwood, Edinburgh and London, 1970). Gilbert Waterhouse, *A Short History of German Literature*, 3rd edn. continued to 1958 by H. M. Waidson (Methuen, London, 1959).

ESSAYS ON INDIVIDUAL AUTHORS

Michael Hamburger, *Reason and Energy. Studies in German Literature* (Weidenfeld & Nicolson, London, 1971). *German Men of Letters*, 6 vols. Vols. 1, 2, 3, 5, A. Natan (ed.). Vol. 4, B. Keith-Smith (ed.). Vol. 6, B. Keith-Smith and A. Natan (eds.) (Wolff, London, 1961–72). *Swiss Men of Letters*, A. Natan (ed.) (Wolff, London, 1970).

ANTHOLOGIES

Patrick Bridgwater (ed.), *Twentieth Century German Verse* (Penguin Books, London, 1963). Leonard Forster (ed.), *The Penguin Book of German Verse* (Penguin Books, London, 1957). Michael Hamburger and Christopher Middleton (eds.), *Modern German Poetry 1910–60* (MacGibbon & Kee, London, 1962). Michael Hamburger (ed.), *East German Poetry. An Anthology in German and English* (Carcanet Press, Oxford, 1972). Christopher Middleton (ed.), *German Writing Today* (Penguin Books, London, 1967). Siegbert Prawer (ed.), *Seventeen Modern German Poets* (Clarendon Press, Oxford, 1971). William Rose (ed.), *A Book of Modern German Lyric Verse 1890–1955* (Clarendon Press, Oxford, 1960). Ernest Stahl (ed.), *The Oxford Book of German Verse*, 3rd edn. (Clarendon Press, Oxford, 1967).

GENRES

E. K. Bennett, *A History of the German Novelle*, 2nd edn., revised and enlarged by H. M. Waidson (Cambridge U.P., Cambridge, 1961). Roy Pascal, *The German Novel* (Manchester U.P., Manchester, 1956). H. M. Waidson, *The Modern German Novel 1945–65*, 2nd edn. (Oxford U.P., London, 1971).

August Closs, *The Genius of the German Lyric*, 2nd edn. (Allen & Unwin, London, 1962). R. D. Gray, *An Introduction to German Poetry* (Cambridge U.P., Cambridge, 1965). Siegbert Prawer, *German Lyric Poetry. A Critical Analysis of Selected Poems from Klopstock to Rilke* (Routledge & Kegan Paul, London, 1952).

W. H. Bruford, *Theatre, Drama and Audience in Goethe's Germany* (Routledge & Kegan Paul, London, 1950). H. F. Garten, *Modern German Drama*, 2nd edn. (Methuen, London, 1964). J. Osborne, *The Naturalist Drama in Germany* (Manchester U.P., Manchester, 1971.) John Prudhoe, *The Theatre of Goethe and Schiller* (Blackwell, Oxford, 1973).

THE MIDDLE AGES

Surveys: Paul B. Salmon, *Literature in Medieval Germany (Introductions to German Literature*, vol. 1). M. O'C. Walshe, *Medieval German Literature* (Harvard U.P., Cambridge, Mass; Oxford U.P., London, 1962).

Epic Poetry: A. T. Hatto, trans., *The Nibelungenlied* (Penguin Books, London, 1965). D. G. Mowatt and Hugh Sacker, *The Nibelungenlied. An Interpretative Commentary* (Toronto U.P. and Clarendon Press, Oxford, 1967). A. T. Hatto, trans., *Gottfried von Strassburg: Tristan* (Penguin Books, London, 1960). W. T. H. Jackson, *The Anatomy of Love. The Tristan of Gottfried von Strassburg* (Columbia U.P., New York and London, 1971). H. M. Mustard and C. E. Passage, trans., *Wolfram von Eschenbach: Parzival* (Vintage Books, New York, 1961). Hugh Sacker, *An Introduction to Wolfram's Parzival* (Cambridge U.P., Cambridge, 1963).

Minnesang: A. T. Hatto and R. J. Taylor, *The Songs of Neidhart von Reuenthal* (Manchester U.P., Manchester, 1958). Olive Sayce, *Poets of the Minnesang* (Clarendon Press, Oxford, 1967).

THE SIXTEENTH AND SEVENTEENTH CENTURIES

Roy Pascal, *German Literature in the Sixteenth and Seventeenth Centuries. Renaissance–Reformation–Baroque (Introductions to German Literature*, vol. 2).

THE EIGHTEENTH CENTURY

Surveys: W. H. Bruford, *Germany in the Eighteenth Century. The Social Background to the Literary Revival* (Cambridge U.P., Cambridge, 1935, repr. 1971). W. H. Bruford, *Culture and Society in Classical Weimar* (Cambridge U.P., Cambridge, 1962). Roy Pascal, *The German Sturm und Drang* (Manchester U.P., Manchester, 1953). E. L. Stahl and W. E. Yuill, *German Literature in the Eighteenth and Nineteenth Centuries (Introductions to German Literature*, vol. 3). L. A. Willoughby, *The Classical Age of German Literature* (Clarendon Press, Oxford, 1926, repr. 1966).

Goethe: Barker Fairley, *A Study of Goethe* (Clarendon Press, Oxford, 1947). Barker Fairley, *Goethe's Faust: Six Essays* (Clarendon Press, Oxford, 1953). F. J. Lamport, *A Student's Guide to Goethe* (Heinemann, London, 1971). David Luke (ed.), *Goethe. Selected Verse* (Penguin Books, London, 1969). Ronald Peacock, *Goethe's Major Plays*, 2nd edn. (Manchester U.P., Manchester, 1966). H. S. Reiss, *Goethe's Novels*

(Macmillan, London, 1969). Elizabeth M. Wilkinson and L. A. Willoughby, *Goethe. Poet and Thinker* (Arnold, London, 1962).

Herder: A. Gillies, *Herder* (Blackwell, Oxford, 1945).

Hölderlin: Michael Hamburger (ed.), *Hölderlin. Selected Verse* (Penguin Books, London, 1961). Ronald Peacock, *Hölderlin*, 2nd edn. (Methuen, London, 1973).

Lessing: H. B. Garland, *Lessing. The Founder of Modern German Literature*, 2nd edn. (Macmillan, London, 1962).

Schiller: H. B. Garland, *Schiller. The Dramatic Writer* (Clarendon Press, Oxford, 1969). E. L. Stahl, *Schiller's Drama. Theory and Practice* (Clarendon Press, Oxford, 1954). Ilse Graham, *Schiller's Drama. Talent and Integrity* (Methuen, London, 1974).

ROMANTICISM

Surveys: Lilian R. Furst, *Romanticism in Perspective* (Macmillan, London, 1969). Siegbert Prawer (ed.), *The Romantic Period in Germany* (Weidenfeld & Nicolson, London, 1970). E. L. Stahl and W. E. Yuill, *German Literature in the Eighteenth and Nineteenth Centuries* (*Introductions to German Literature*, vol. 3). Ronald Taylor (ed.), *The Romantic Tradition in Germany. An Anthology* (Methuen, London, 1970). L. A. Willoughby, *The Romantic Movement in German Literature* (Clarendon Press, Oxford, 1930, repr. 1966).

Jacob and Wilhelm Grimm: Ruth Michaelis-Jena, *The Brothers Grimm* (Routledge, London, 1970).

Hoffmann: Ronald Taylor, *Hoffmann* (Bowes & Bowes, London, 1963).

Kleist: E. L. Stahl, *The Dramas of Heinrich von Kleist*, 2nd edn. (Blackwell, Oxford, 1961).

THE NINETEENTH CENTURY

Surveys: Hermann Boeschenstein, *German Literature of the Nineteenth Century* (Arnold, London, 1969). Roy Pascal, *From Naturalism to Expressionism. German Literature and Society, 1880–1918* (Weidenfeld & Nicolson, London, 1973). E. L. Stahl and W. E. Yuill, *German Literature in the Eighteenth and Nineteenth Centuries* (*Introductions to German Literature*, vol. 3).

Essays on individual authors: J. P. Stern, *Re-interpretations. Seven Studies in Nineteenth Century German Literature* (Thames & Hudson, London, 1964). J. P. Stern, *Idylls and Reality. Studies in Nineteenth Century German Literature* (Methuen, London, 1971).

Büchner: A. H. J. Knight, *Georg Büchner* (Blackwell, Oxford, 1951).

Droste-Hülshoff: Margaret Mare, *Annette von Droste-Hülshoff* (Methuen, London, 1965).

George: E. K. Bennett, *Stefan George* (Bowes & Bowes, Cambridge, 1954).

Grillparzer: G. A. Wells, *The Plays of Grillparzer* (Pergamon, London, 1969). W. E. Yates, *Grillparzer. A Critical Introduction* (Cambridge U.P., Cambridge, 1972).

Hauptmann: H. F. Garten, *Gerhart Hauptmann* (Bowes & Bowes, Cambridge, 1954). Margaret Sinden, *Gerhart Hauptmann: the Prose Plays* (Toronto U.P., Toronto, 1957).

Heine: Peter Branscombe (ed.), *Heine. Selected Verse* (Penguin Books, London, 1967). Barker Fairley, *Heinrich Heine. An Interpretation* (Clarendon Press, Oxford, 1954). Laura Hofrichter, *Heinrich Heine* (Clarendon Press, Oxford, 1963). Siegbert Prawer, *Heine the Tragic Satirist* (Cambridge U.P., Cambridge, 1961).

Keller: J. M. Lindsay, *Gottfried Keller. Life and Works* (Wolff, London, 1968).

Meyer: W. D. Williams, *The Stories of C. F. Meyer* (Blackwell, Oxford, 1962).

Mörike: Margaret Mare, *Eduard Mörike. The Man and the Poet* (Methuen, London, 1957).

Nestroy: W. E. Yates, *Nestroy. Satire and Parody in Viennese Popular Comedy* (Cambridge U.P., Cambridge, 1972).

Nietzsche: R. J. Hollingdale, *Nietzsche. The Man and his Philosophy* (Routledge & Kegan Paul, London, 1965).

Raabe: Barker Fairley, *Wilhelm Raabe. An Introduction to his Novels* (Clarendon Press, Oxford, 1961).

Raimund: Dorothy Prohaska, *Raimund and Vienna. A Critical Study of Raimund's Plays in their Viennese Setting* (Cambridge U.P., Cambridge, 1970).

Schnitzler: Martin Swales, *Arthur Schnitzler. A Critical Study* (Clarendon Press, Oxford, 1972).

Stifter: E. A. Blackall, *Adalbert Stifter. A Critical Study* (Cambridge U.P., Cambridge, 1948).

THE TWENTIETH CENTURY

Surveys: August Closs, *Twentieth Century German Literature* (*Introductions to German Literature*, vol. 4). Konrad Franke, *Die Literatur der Deutschen Demokratischen Republik* (Kindler, München and Zürich, 1971). Henry Hatfield, *Modern German Literature* (Arnold, London, 1966). Theodore Huebener, *The Literature of East Germany* (Ungar, New York, 1970). R. S. Furness, *Expressionism* (*The Critical Idiom*, vol. 29) (Methuen, London, 1973). John Willett, *Expressionism* (Weidenfeld & Nicholson, London, 1971).

Bobrowski: Brian Keith-Smith, *Johannes Bobrowski* (*Modern German Authors. Texts and Contexts* R. W. Last (ed.), vol. 4 (Wolff, London, 1970). Ruth and Matthew Mead, trans., *Johannes Bobrowski and Horst Bienek. Selected Poems* (Penguin Books, London, 1971).

Böll: Enid Macpherson, *Heinrich Böll* (Heinemann, London, 1971). James H. Reid, *Heinrich Böll* (Wolff, London, 1973).

Brecht: Martin Esslin, *Brecht. A Choice of Evils* (Eyre & Spottiswoode, London, 1959). John Willett, *The Theatre of Bertolt Brecht*, 3rd edn. (Methuen, London, 1967).

Celan: Siegbert Prawer, 'Paul Celan' (*German Men of Letters*, vol. 4).

Grass: A. V. Subiotto, 'Günter Grass' (*German Men of Letters*, vol. 4).

Hesse: G. W. Field, *Hermann Hesse* (Twayne, New York, 1970). Theodore Ziolkowski, *The Novels of Hermann Hesse* (Princeton U.P., Oxford U.P., London, 1965).

Kafka: Ronald Gray, *Franz Kafka* (Cambridge U.P., Cambridge, 1973). John Hibberd, *Franz Kafka. A Biographical Introduction* (Studio Vista, London, 1974). Anthony Thorlby, *Kafka. A Study* (Heinemann, London, 1972).

Thomas Mann: Erich Heller, *The Ironic German. A Study of Thomas Mann* (Secker & Warburg, London, 1958). R. J. Hollingdale, *Thomas Mann. A Critical Study* (Hart-Davis, London, 1971). R. Hinton Thomas, *Thomas Mann. The Mediation of Art* (Clarendon Press, Oxford, 1956).

Rilke: E. M. Butler, *Rainer Maria Rilke* (Cambridge U.P., Cambridge, 1946). E. C. Mason, *Rilke* (Oliver & Boyd, Edinburgh and London, 1963).

Trakl: T. J. Casey, *Manshape that Shone. An Interpretation of Trakl* (Blackwell, Oxford, 1964). H. Lindenberger, *Georg Trakl* (Twayne, New York, 1971). Christopher Middleton (ed.), *Georg Trakl. Selected Poems* (Cape, London, 1968).

Index